AGAINST THE ODDS

My most improbable win: Arcangues and the Breeders' Cup Classic—at 99 to 1.

AGAINST THE ODDS

Riding for My Life

JERRY BAILEY

with Tom Pedulla

G. P. Putnam's Sons   *New York*

G. P. PUTNAM'S SONS
Publishers Since 1838
Published by the Penguin Group
Penguin Group (USA) Inc., 375 Hudson Street, New York, New York 10014, USA • Penguin Group
(Canada) 10 Alcorn Avenue, Toronto, Ontario M4V 3B2, Canada (a division of Pearson Penguin
Canada Inc.) • Penguin Books Ltd, 80 Strand, London WC2R 0RL, England • Penguin Ireland,
25 St Stephen's Green, Dublin 2, Ireland (a division of Penguin Books Ltd) • Penguin Group (Australia),
250 Camberwell Road, Camberwell, Victoria 3124, Australia (a division of Pearson Australia Group
Pty Ltd) • Penguin Books India Pvt Ltd, 11 Community Centre, Panchsheel Park, New Delhi 110 017,
India • Penguin Group (NZ), Cnr Airborne and Rosedale Roads, Albany, Auckland 1310,
New Zealand (a division of Pearson New Zealand Ltd) • Penguin Books (South Africa) (Pty) Ltd,
24 Sturdee Avenue, Rosebank, Johannesburg 2196, South Africa • Penguin Books Ltd,
Registered Offices: 80 Strand, London WC2R 0RL, England

Library of Congress Cataloging-in-Publication Data

Bailey, Jerry, date.
Against the odds : riding for my life / Jerry Bailey, with Tom Pedulla.
p.   cm.
ISBN 0-399-15273-3
1. Bailey, Jerry.   2. Jockeys—United States—Biography.   I. Pedulla, Tom.   II. Title.
SF336.B35B35   2005   2004058640
798.4'0092—dc22
[B]

Printed in the United States of America
1   3   5   7   9   10   8   6   4   2

This book is printed on acid-free paper. ∞

Book design by Meighan Cavanaugh

To my loving wife and best friend, Suzee,

whose love and strength saw me through my lowest lows

and helped me reach my highest highs.

CONTENTS

One
_____

SWIMMING TOWARD THE LIGHT

I had hit bottom.

My descent into alcoholism had been slow, with movements so subtle as to be almost imperceptible at times. But now it felt as though I was lying at the bottom of the ocean, searching for a ray of light that would lead me to the surface.

I needed to breathe again. I needed to live again. In the afternoon, I was one of the world's most prominent jockeys. But I'd sneak a shot in the morning to keep me from trembling, and after the last race, the floodgates would open. I no longer wanted to continue that lie.

I no longer wanted to return home to demean and berate my loving wife, Suzee. She would eagerly await my arrival, only to fall back into her despair when she saw my drunkenness once again. Through slurred speech, I would abuse her verbally, psychologically, often until she fled the house for long, tearful drives into the night.

I should have worried about it during those times when she put the miles and me behind her. I should have done something, anything, to keep her from leaving instead of hurling more insults as she disappeared from view.

Instead, I rejoiced. Time for another drink or two or three—with no one to stop me.

As I sat at my first Alcoholics Anonymous meeting in January 1989, I wondered how I had ever become so sick. It had started innocently, when I set out on my riding career in 1974 at the up-for-anything age of seventeen.

All I'd wanted to do was fit in, to experience the off-track camaraderie. So I drank, first because it allowed me to be part of the party, and in later years because . . . well, I am not sure exactly why. All I know is that the more I realized I needed to stop, the more powerless I felt to do so.

That will sound strange to those who know all that I have accomplished since my first day of sobriety, on January 15, 1989. The world at large cannot imagine how a man widely declared to be the leading rider of his era, one of the greatest jockeys ever to break from the starting gate, could have handled a 1,200-pound Thoroughbred with so much ease but have no control of himself

The world at large cannot imagine how a man who would go on to be a Hall of Famer and win every major race there is more than once—the Kentucky Derby, Preakness and Belmont Stakes twice each; four Breeders' Cup Classics, four Dubai World

Cups—could have started as such a loser away from the eyes of the admiring crowd.

The world at large cannot imagine how a man who would win an unprecedented seven Eclipse awards as the nation's outstanding jockey from 1995 to 2003, who would set earnings records every year from 2001 to 2003, who would set yet another record, this time for stakes victories, in 2003, could have lost his way so badly.

The smaller world that is composed of alcoholics and other substance abusers, they can relate.

They can understand New Year's Day 1989. Suzee had spent New Year's Eve at her parents' house in Tampa, desiring, I suspect, to be away from me as much as she wanted to be with them.

She called to wish me a Happy New Year. I was passed out on the couch and very much alone. I don't recall what I said, but I remember being unable to speak clearly. If I had to guess, I'd bet that I probably assured her that I had not been drinking, even as I stumbled over my words. When I hung up the phone, we both knew how pathetic I had become.

Alcoholics can relate to the confrontation we had when she returned from Tampa to the house we had rented while I was competing in South Florida. For months now I had been insisting to my wife that I had stopped drinking and was regularly attending Alcoholics Anonymous meetings.

Well, she'd decided to test me. The owners had left behind half a gallon of gin in a kitchen cabinet. Unbeknownst to me, she had marked the bottle to reflect the amount that was in it. Now, I couldn't stand the taste of gin, but I assure you that didn't stop me.

Suzee found the half-gallon container nearly empty and confronted me with it. She was on the attack and threatened to leave me. I had heard that before. This night, though, there was something in her voice that told me she could not hang in there any longer. She was fighting for me, but I had done nothing to save myself.

Denials were not possible. The gin was almost gone. I was convinced she would leave me forever if she heard more empty promises. I had hit bottom and dragged her down with me.

For a change, I told the truth. I confessed that my drinking had gone on unabated. As for the AA meetings I had told her about, I admitted I had twice a week gone as far as the entrance to the church where they were held. And no farther.

I was crying. She was crying. The maternal instincts that had been frustrated while we struggled through infertility problems during the early years of our marriage surfaced. She cradled me in her arms like an infant, and that's how helpless I felt. In our desperation, I called Fred Maas, a police officer in Metro-Dade, Florida.

"I need to talk," I told him.

"I'll be right over," he promised.

And he was. We had been friends for more than a decade, and he was someone I could confide in. I explained to him my reluctance to enter an inpatient program because that would keep me from my riding assignments and force me to go public with my disease. I feared that owners and trainers would suddenly take a dim view of me and make sure I did not go anywhere near their finest Thoroughbreds. That would all but ruin my career.

Fred told me about an outpatient program run by Terry Grant in South Miami. It would require a seven-day-a-week commitment, but I was more than ready. The moment I walked into the room, I knew I belonged.

There were approximately twenty-five other patients in that room, including a doctor, a lawyer, a sanitation worker, and someone from just about every walk of life in between. Alcoholism sweeps across all social and economic lines, making sure every one of its victims pays an equally steep price.

I had hoped no one would recognize me—but the first person I saw was someone who worked at the track. I didn't really care, though. I needed help, I absolutely had to have help, and right then it didn't much matter to me who knew it. Fortunately, he respected my privacy as I would eventually protect that of other celebrities.

I soon found that the mental strain of admitting my problem would be followed by the physical. The first night of my sobriety, my body craved alcohol. I went to bed and woke up in a heavy sweat. The sheets were soaked. I was shaking uncontrollably. Suzee held me close and kept me as still as she could.

At least she knew I was truly staying away from the bottle this time. That night, despite our fitful sleep, we felt a tranquillity together that we had not experienced before.

We both had so many questions about what would be involved in our new beginning. While I was familiarizing myself with the program, Suzee and I invited Terry to dinner at a Chinese restaurant in Miami Beach. He explained to her that alcoholism was not just my disease but one that had afflicted our whole family. At first, she wasn't buying it.

"I don't have the problem," she shot back. "He does."

Terry patiently explained that the success of the program depended on her willingness to attend meetings just as much as it depended on my commitment. After all, she had denied the problem for a long time. When I had struggled with my speech and staggered around shortly after we got married, she blamed it on a blood sugar imbalance due to a jockey's limited food intake. I, of course, was quick to agree with that assessment.

Now, we could fool each other no longer. We were staring at the truth, and neither one of us could afford to look away.

"You are going to be glad you are married to an alcoholic when all of this is over," Terry reassured her.

She still looked like she wasn't buying it.

After that dinner, I participated in my first AA meeting. I was a good listener, but I was reluctant to speak. My first sponsor urged me to change that. "If you don't talk at the meetings, you're wasting your gas money," he said.

I was not going to let the second meeting pass me by. We held hands and went around in a circle, each participant introducing himself or herself and telling how alcoholism had diminished his or her life. Finally, it was my turn.

Terry had prepared me for the moment by giving me the option of identifying myself by my first name only and omitting any mention of my disease. But I knew what had to be done as surely as I know when an opening must be seized in a race. I did not hesitate.

"Hi, my name is Jerry," I told the group, "and I'm an alcoholic."

My friends and family think it must have been agonizing to utter those words. It wasn't. It was a huge relief. I had been hiding the truth for so long. Now I was finally confronting my demons. For the first time I fully understood what they mean when they say, "The truth will set you free." A wonderful sense of that freedom accompanied my admission, an elation that topped any trip to the winner's circle. After years of false promises and broken vows, I finally meant what I said.

While I had hit bottom and the ocean was deep, there was comfort in that. There was only one direction to take now. It was up to me to swim toward the light, and I was kicking as hard as I could.

Two

THE RIGHT FIT

I was twelve years old when my tumultuous ride began. The "track" was nothing more than an open field, bordered on two sides by a drainage ditch, in my hometown of El Paso, Texas. The name of my opponent, a neighborhood acquaintance, has faded from my memory.

The nervous anticipation that I experienced for the first time, that I would feel before so many major races in my career, will always remain vivid. Athletes crave that rush, that overwhelming sense of being on edge, that uncertainty of what is about to unfold.

There would not be much strategy in this race. The clearing was only a hundred yards or so long. This was about the faster horse—and the braver boy.

We were off in an instant. My butterflies vanished as soon as I felt the surge of power beneath me. I was immediately riding hard, pushing on my horse's neck, asking him to give me almost everything he had. The hunched figure beside me was equally hell-bent, and they were matching us stride for stride. We would inch ahead, he would respond. His horse would thrust his nose in front, we would fight back.

Time to go to the whip, to find that little extra that would make the difference. I reached high with my right hand—and missed my horse's butt entirely. I struggled to regain my balance and hang on. Handling a stick looked so easy on television.

Although the outcome was too close to call, the impact of that afternoon had nothing to do with which horse covered the length of a football field the fastest. The feeling of the wind against my face, the sight of the finish drawing ever closer, the sound of horse and rider straining to reach there first—this was something I wanted to do again and again.

This was something I wanted to do for the rest of my life.

If our horses had been up to it, we would have squared off ten more times that afternoon. Once was enough to tell me everything I needed to know.

Racing is filled with rags-to-riches stories. While I would encounter enough adversity to break most men, I was hardly the victim of a deprived childhood. My father, Jim, was a successful dentist, and my mother, Betty, met our needs, and then some. And while I butted heads almost every day with my older sister, Becky, and my younger sister, Kathy, we loved one another.

My father kept a string of horses out back, but ironically, in our early years, my sisters showed more interest in them than I did. They used to enjoy long, leisurely rides into the woods with our parents. Not me. If I could not go fast, I did not want to go at all.

KATHY: *He started seeing he could go fast. He always liked to do everything fast. He played the piano fast, he did his chores fast, he drove fast. The speed element had a lot to do with his getting into the sport. It just rang his bell.*

At first I preferred to play football and basketball with the guys in our neighborhood, but there was just one problem—actually two. You need bulk for football, height for basketball. Since my father stood five-five and my mother five-one, it was not a shock that I was soon left behind on the growth chart and increasingly left out of pickup games.

I wanted so much to excel, and yet no amount of desire could compensate for the essentials I lacked. The gap in size between me and my classmates kept getting bigger. When I was nine or ten, all of the kids really started opening up on me, and by the time I reached high school, the difference was dramatic.

I could not find football pads small enough to fit me. By the time I reached seventh grade at Zack White Elementary School, there was no point in even trying out for the team. I could not endure the embarrassment anymore. If there was room for ten players, there were twelve who were bigger and better than me. It added to my exasperation that almost all of them were my friends.

Dubb White, the football coach, saw how much I wanted to be included, and he took me on as a manager. I was one step above a water boy as I taped ankles and made sure the equipment was ready—but I was part of the team. In football-crazed Texas, that made me a big deal. Or at least I felt that way.

I managed the basketball team as well, and when I wasn't doing that, I shot baskets outside our garage. I would do it for two or three hours at a time, almost always by myself, alone with my imagination, because I knew that if I played with my lanky friends, I would get my brains beaten in. The fierce competitor in me would not allow that. Better to practice, I thought, than to play and lose.

I would shoot jump shots before dinner, eat quickly, then take more jumpers. A light attached to the garage allowed me to dribble and drive long after dark—and wonder if I might ever be competitive.

When I reached Coronado High School in El Paso, there were three directions to choose from in terms of running buddies. You had your athletes, your book kids, and your wild ones. The nerds did not interest me. The other groups sure did.

My desperation to letter as an athlete led me to join the wrestling team as a sophomore. In that sport, my 105 pounds was no hindrance at all, since I wrestled with others in the same weight class, and my competitiveness helped me win more matches than I lost. I was not a state champ or anything, but I did well enough.

At the end of the season, I lined up with my teammates and received a big gold "C" on a blue background. It still means as much to me now as many of the racing trophies I've won.

I also cherished my friendship with a boy named Kevin Baker, not so much for who he was but for what he did for me. He was the captain of the football team, and when he welcomed me into his circle, I gained acceptance throughout the school. Of course there was something in it for Kevin as well. My father kept a keg of beer on tap at our house at all times. Kevin, his teammates and I could get pretty thirsty.

I was a fast learner and achieved top grades, even though I was drawn to competition, not books. When I was not playing, I was working. Despite our comfortable upbringing, my parents did a great job of teaching us that if you wanted something, you had better work for it.

And if you were going to do something, do it right. If we got it wrong, we immediately heard about it. If we got it right—well, I don't remember hearing about that. Words of praise were not heard very often in the Bailey household, if ever. There was not a lot of confidence-building going on.

We were never spoiled. My dad made sure of that. He had entered North Texas State on a boxing scholarship in 1949, and that says plenty about him. He was a lightweight in classification only.

JIM: *I liked it because I was on my own. If I won, it was my win. If I lost, it was my loss.*

I enjoyed trying to outthink the other guy, how to get a step on him. When we were sitting on our stools, I would try to think about what would make him quit.

I started boxing in high school to be accepted by the bigger guys. I never admitted that to anyone, but it was true. I stopped after I broke my hand for a second time and turned my attention to dentistry.

My dad would do whatever it took to succeed, even if it meant absorbing a beating. I was the same way.

I would wake up shortly after daybreak to muck the stalls, then I would make sure our horses were cleaned and fed. If the lawn needed to be mowed, that was my chore. If the garden needed attention, my name was on that, too. It was a lot of work for a few dollars a week, but that was what my father expected. I was not about to disappoint him.

On many evenings, I accompanied my father to the driving range to shag golf balls for him. I would use my baseball glove to catch the balls in the air. It was great fun for me, plenty frustrating on the other end, though. A golfer wants to know his total yardage. My father only knew what he got on the fly. Still, I was a bargain since I received only twenty-five cents for every fifty balls. As for the time I spent waiting outside while my father drank to excess with his buddies and played cards, he did not give a damn about that.

Sometimes, I was as much a trial for my parents as they were for me. One day, they were watching as I rode Red on our property. He was an arthritic, stiff-going horse, but as kind as a kitten. We got along great except for this one time, when poor Red stumbled and fell. I hit the ground so hard it knocked the breath out of me. My parents rushed to my side. I was moaning and groaning, and my mother feared I was dying. The thought of having another dentist in the family grew pretty appealing to her after that.

As for me, the accident was no big deal. It never occurred to me that I would not climb aboard again. As soon as I recovered my breath, I was ready to find Red and go for another spin.

That spirit landed me a job in the mornings working for a trainer named J. J. Pletcher at Sunland Park, New Mexico, a short drive from El Paso. There I met Ray York, one of a number of people who would influence my career.

Ray immediately gained my attention and admiration. While he had fallen into relative obscurity and was now just an exercise rider, he boasted that one line in his résumé that motivates everyone associated with the racetrack—from owner to trainer to jockey to groom—to jump out of bed before dawn. Ray had ridden in the Kentucky Derby five times. He had smelled the roses and, better than that, had won with a driving victory aboard Determine in 1954.

If I could have switched my brain and Ray's, I would have. I wanted his knowledge, all of it or as much as he was willing to pass on. Fortunately for me, he was generous with his time. I will always be indebted to him for that.

"Stay as close to the pace as possible," Ray would tell me, "without using up your horse. Save something for the end."

"Pace makes the race" is one of the axioms of the sport. Ray taught me all about pace. A rider develops a clock in his head that gives him an idea of how swiftly his horse is traveling every furlong, an eighth of a mile.

If you wonder about that, think of it this way. Experienced highway drivers develop clocks in their heads without even realizing it. They know what fifty-five or sixty-five miles per hour feels like. They maintain that speed with relative ease.

Horses are far more complicated than a gentle push on the accelerator, but they give their riders cues, and their body language tells the jockey how comfortable he is traveling at certain speeds. Then the rider must calculate the rate at which he is covering the ground and measure out that speed to, as Ray would say, save something for the end.

That clock in the rider's head is developed through nothing more complicated than repetition. Since every morning work is timed, you always know your speed. If they say you went four furlongs, or half a mile, in 48 seconds—12-second clips are desirable in prepping good horses—you know what it felt like. If five furlongs required one minute, you have an image of that in your mind.

Your sense of time becomes sharper and sharper. Since horses have different strides, pace can be felt by how quickly you reach different portions of the track. Again, it is like driving a car, and not nearly as complex as it sounds. Your surroundings tell you your speeds. Often, the person timing does not even need to tell you how a work went. You already know.

One other thing: When a trainer instructs you to drill a horse in a certain time, you had better hit that mark or be damn close to it. Too fast a work can leave a horse empty when it counts; go too slow and he may not be sharp enough to meet the demands ahead. There is no margin for error at the racetrack.

As the school year ended, J. J. Pletcher shifted his stable to Centennial Park in Littleton, Colorado, and invited me to continue working for him there. I was all of fifteen, very much a man of the world in my opinion, and I did not have to think about it.

Ignoring my mother's protestations, I bought a huge green Army trunk which, for reasons unknown, I painted bright orange. I stuffed all of my clothes in there as well as a hot plate and a pan. I loaded it onto a bus bound for Denver and watched El Paso recede into the distance.

Although I probably should have thought twice, I felt no trepidation about leaving home. I was ready and eager. All my life, I had been viewed as a kid who had it made because his father was a dentist, because "Daddy would always deliver." I was out to show the world I could make it on my own.

Those kinds of thoughts added to the jumble in my head as that bus groaned its way to Denver. It seemed as though it took forever, but it was actually only a day and a night. When I hurried off the bus, J.J., his wife, Jerrie, and his son, Todd—who would go on to become one of racing's most prominent trainers—were there to greet me.

Convenience ended there. I lived in a tack room at the end of the barn, a short distance from the four horses I was responsible for grooming. Although they were far from champions, I did everything in my power to make them glitter. I would graze them in late afternoon almost until sunset, knowing that the nutrition provided by lush, fresh grass would help their coats dapple and shine. I wanted them looking their best.

I was doing this for them and also for myself. None of the other backstretch workers knew I came from a well-to-do background. I was simply one of them. I was making thirty dollars a week and considered a warm meal to be a can of Campbell's soup prepared on my hot plate. When I had an appetite for meat, I made do with a bologna sandwich. I was putting away money for a car. I had my priorities.

J.J. allowed me to work a few horses at the end of training hours each day, and I became fond of a large bay with a good disposition and an unpromising nickname: Slow Motion.

One day, J.J. instructed me to breeze Slow Motion half a mile under the watchful eye of the clocker. When we returned to the barn from the track, he was there to greet us.

"Did you get a time on him?"

"They told me I went in fifty-two [seconds]."

"You couldn't shoot this horse out of a cannon in fifty-two," J.J. said incredulously.

"J.J., that's what they told me."

And that was the time of the work. While it did not rank with the strongest performances that day, it still represented a lifetime best for a horse who was typically listless in the morning and all but comatose in the afternoon.

Immediately, I thought I had a gift. I'd made Slow Motion go faster than he ever had before. It gave me hope. I'd felt good on him, and he had responded to me.

After being thrown aside like a sack of dirty laundry on the football field, and getting my soft jump shots hurled back at me on the basketball court, perhaps I finally had what it took to succeed in a sport.

Further inspiration came one day when I saw Bobby Salas, the stable jockey, motor up to the barn in his new maroon Monte Carlo. That big car gleamed with an out-of-the-showroom shine. As for the buxom girl on Bobby's arm, well, my hormones had been raging even before I laid eyes on her.

I guarantee Bobby wasn't a speck taller than four-ten, but when I looked at him, the car, and the babe, he seemed larger than life. I said to myself, "Man, that's what I want to do. This guy has got it made."

My great adventure that summer came after my parents visited in August. Both of them had slipped me money, and I was eager to put some of that into a birthday present for Mom. Although I had never driven anything other than my father's tractor, I talked Rigo, the foreman, into lending me his five-speed truck so I could visit a nearby mall.

If I was crazy for asking, he must have been crazier for agreeing. I looked like I was twelve. I was an arrest waiting to happen. He gave me the keys, though, and I stacked a couple of telephone books on the seat so I could see above the dashboard. I reached the mall, took care of Mom's present, eyed a few girls, and perched on those telephone books again for the drive back, all without being caught. This was the exclamation point to that very good summer.

I returned home for my junior year at Coronado High and continued to work horses in the morning. They were cheap, sore animals at the bottom of the claiming ranks. They felt fine to me, though, and they were invaluable as instructors. Horses will tell you their wants and needs. You just have to be smart enough to pay attention.

I reached a crossroads in the spring of 1974, when J.J. asked if I wanted to become his foreman. It was a great compliment and a huge responsibility. I was sixteen, cocky on the outside but not so sure inside.

I came home to my dad and told him about the offer. "It's your choice," my father began, in the way he positioned everything for us, "but do you want to be a foreman or do you want to be a jockey?"

With one sentence, he crystallized my future for me.

"I want to be a jockey," I replied.

I plunged headlong into that pursuit in the summer. I headed to Santa Fe Downs in New Mexico, where exercise riders were at a premium. I would work as many as I could fit in during training hours, which extended from 5:30 A.M to 10 A.M.

The pay was two dollars a head. I never missed a morning or an opportunity. Taking a day off never entered my mind. This was not work at all. It was fun. Why would I take a day off from fun?

Those outside the racing world cannot understand how trainers and their help report day after day and hardly ever take a break. Vacations are almost unheard of. The explanation is actually very simple. When you love horses, when you are passionate about what you do, you never want to leave.

When I turned sixteen, I celebrated in style. My father and I took a short flight to Dallas, where I purchased my grandmother's white 1961 Chevy Impala. The flight cost more than the Impala, which I bought for all of one hundred dollars before I drove it home.

"Son," my father told me, "this car has probably never been over fifty-five miles per hour, so don't gut it."

You can guess the first thing I did. There was nothing sleek about that four-door Impala, but believe me, that speedometer pushed past fifty-five.

I was wild. I didn't know if the drinking age was eighteen or twenty-one, and I didn't care. I never paid much attention to regulations, whether they pertained to speed limit or age limit. I did know you needed to be older than sixteen. But that never stopped me from imbibing with my racetrack friends.

If there was a party, I was there. So was alcohol. We drank lots of beer, and I didn't even like the taste. Peer pressure dictated that I not sit there empty-handed. After feeling left out of pickup games as a youngster, I was prepared to do almost anything to be liked, to be part of this scene.

Finally, I belonged.

Three

WINS, AND ONE
HUGE LOSS

*T*hen, on November 2, 1974, I received an unforgettable phone call.

It was Ike Danley, one of the trainers who had overseen my development as an exercise rider.

Ike asked, "Can you come ride a horse for me?"

"Like today?" I blurted.

"Like now," he responded. "My jockey took off sick."

He didn't have to ask me twice.

I grabbed my riding boots and helmet and hustled to Sunland Park for a sudden date with Pegged Rate.

It all happened so fast there was no time for nervousness. The next thing I knew, we were in the gate, the bell rang, and we were off. Pegged Rate and I left the starting gate in good order and settled in the middle of the pack; then I glanced to my left and spotted an opening on the rail. I squeezed Pegged Rate into it, allowing us to work our way into contention.

My adrenaline was pumping now. Maybe we could win! In my first race! I asked Pegged Rate for more . . . and nothing happened. In an instant, I felt as useless as the rider who had taken off sick. The horse had nothing left. We dropped back as steadily as we had advanced, and finished no better than eighth.

That's a lucid description, but believe me, the whole experience was a big blur. Everything had been going two hundred miles per hour, and I'd felt helpless to slow it down. At my father's urging, I had resisted the temptation to become an apprentice earlier, even though many friends had thought I was ready, and now I knew what he meant. Exercising horses is nothing like racing them. The strength required, and the instantaneous decision-making, is a whole different deal.

As if I wasn't shaken enough by my initial start, an encounter with a jockey named Larry Byers added to my brief but difficult afternoon. Larry was probably forty at the time, although he looked twice that age. Too many mornings and afternoons of toiling under a blistering sun had left him with leathery skin—and I imagine too many late nights explained the deep, dark circles under his eyes. His foul-smelling breath spoke of a lifetime of tobacco use.

"Kid," Larry told me, "next time you come through a hole like that, you'd better say something."

"Okay." I nodded. But inside I was thinking, *What the hell is he talking about?* I approached him after the next race and asked for an explanation.

"I was setting a trap for somebody," he said, "and it wasn't you."

Vengeance, with the idea of beating another rider but not injuring him, plays a prominent role at the racetrack. Larry had created that hole with the intention of shutting it down on a specific person as payback for a perceived earlier slight. Then I had come along, just in time to spoil his grand plan.

I'm sure he set another trap on another day. Jockeys do not forget. Those who allow themselves to be victims of rough riding without exacting some consequence do not last very long. Larry was never one to back off, thus his longevity.

As for me, I would get another chance the very next day at Sunland. That was when my debut had been scheduled all along, before Pegged Rate's jockey had come down sick. I was to ride Fetch in the co-feature and Roniway in the last race. My father had helped to line up the mounts.

JIM: *He couldn't get an agent to take his book. They said, "You're from a rich family. You're not going to be riding in a year." I said, "You're missing out."*

I helped him with his book a bit. I didn't know a dadgum thing about being an agent. I would say, "Put my son on your horse. He will give you an honest ride." I didn't say which horse. I was just trying to get him started.

Fortunately, my first two scheduled starters, both for Ike Danley, were live ones. Ike assured me I had done nothing wrong on Pegged Rate—the horse was not nearly good enough. No pilot can make the difference when there's not enough engine beneath him.

Fetch inspired confidence in Ike, however. "Just keep him out of trouble," he said. "Don't get too close to the other horses' heels." In other words, don't get yourself killed.

Fetch took great care of me, and I did not make any mistakes during a mile that felt like a furlong. Everything went very smoothly. There was nothing complicated about that race. We were always not far off the pace, always in striking position. I turned him loose down the stretch. And we won by three and a half lengths—and at a price, too. Perhaps due to my inexperience, Fetch rewarded his backers with $21.40 for a $2 win bet.

My first victory felt surreal. I hadn't even realized until I watched the television replay that when Fetch had lugged in at one point, I switched the whip from my right to my left hand and quickly put him on a straight course again. My years of preparation had made such a maneuver instinctual, and I delighted in that.

My strongest memory of that race is that my legs almost came out from under me when I dismounted. They felt so rubbery they practically buckled. Fortunately, I was spared that embarrassment in front of my parents, my sisters, and eight or ten high school friends who had come out to cheer me on.

There was joy, but no great display of emotion and certainly no tears. That was not my family's style.

KATHY: *They provided well for us and raised us very well, but Dad was not raised to be emotional or affectionate and nor was Mom.*

JIM: *I congratulated him. As a parent, you are a victim of the way you were raised. We weren't gushy, loving people. My parents were very distant. I never saw them hug or kiss or anything.*

My big day was not over. I still had Roniway. He presented a stiffer challenge because he was known for drifting wide around turns, but I clutched my stick in my right hand and used it to keep him in line. He needed just a few taps. We won by three-quarters of a length, paying $14.80 this time.

Two for two! I can still see my parents walking proudly to greet me for the second time. "Doc," track announcer Harry Henson called out to my father in a booming voice from his upstairs booth, "it looks like you have a real good one there."

My father's cowboy hat seemed to fill the winner's circle. If I'd bothered to focus on it, my mother's wig would have stood out, too. The wig disguised a reality I was trying hard to push to the back of my mind while I focused on my career.

She had recently discovered a lump in her right breast and undergone surgery for cancer that had spread to her lymph nodes. A vigorous program of chemotherapy was already debilitating her in many ways, including the loss of her hair.

Mom never let on that her illness was all that difficult. Perhaps that made it easier for us to act as if it was almost nonexistent. The truth, one that I will always regret, is that I all but ignored the gravity of the situation.

BECKY: *We all thought she was going to be okay, probably because we wanted her to be okay so badly.*

JIM: *I talked to an oncologist in Houston, which had one of the best cancer treatment centers in the United States, but I feel guilty because I wasn't able to do more for Betty. The surgeons told me, "Jim, this is an overwhelming type of cancer. You're doing everything*

*that can be done." That didn't ease my tremendous sense of failure,
though.*

KATHY: *Everybody kind of headed his own way. Jerry was riding
and doing his thing. My sister was doing her thing. I focused on
cheerleading in high school. Dad was working and taking care
of Mom.*

I brought home nine winners in the last two months of 1974. I
was on my way.

Mom declined steadily in the early months of the following
year. She was too ill to attend my races. We set up a radio next to
her bed, and it was as if the race calls provided a reprieve from
the cancer cells that were overtaking her body.

At first, she asked me which mounts I liked the most, and bet
accordingly. Pretty soon, she stopped asking. Riding and select-
ing winners are very different skills. If I could square off against
the best jockeys of all time, I would relish the challenge. I have
never been very good when it comes to predictions, though.

Mom decided on a standard six-dollar bet—two dollars to
win, two dollars to place, two dollars to show—and always made
that wager regardless of whether I was on the favorite or a seemingly hopeless long shot. We later found $1,700 she'd made in
successful wagers safely tucked away.

Mom was in and out of the hospital. She underwent a hys-
terectomy. She required blood transfusions. Toward the end,
morphine drips were needed to control her pain. Then there was
no controlling her pain.

To this day I regret that I continued putting myself first. After
graduating early from high school as an above-average student, I

planned my summer as if I did not have a care in the world. Where was I going to ride? What could I do to advance?

I never gave a thought to staying home with Mom.

How could I have been so selfish? I will never know the answer to that question, one that will stay with me for the rest of my life and that never fails to bring tears to my eyes. I was self-centered to the end.

That end came on Mother's Day 1975. I did not visit her at the hospital after flying in from Omaha to ride at Sunland Park. I called. "I'm doing pretty good," she said. "Go ride and come back to the hospital when you are finished."

That was all I needed to hear. Dad accompanied me to the track and we immersed ourselves in that day's race card until he was paged before the fourth race. "Your mom is not doing good," he said. "Do you want to go with me?"

We left immediately, but not soon enough. Mom's assurances that she was "doing pretty good" were the last words she would ever speak to me. She had fallen in the bathroom and lapsed into a coma a few minutes after that.

Although her husband and three children pressed close to her, hoping to tell her how much we loved her, wanting her to know how much she would always be part of us, she would never regain consciousness.

BECKY: *I think she knew we were there because her breathing would change. We would say something or touch her hand and her breathing would become a little more labored.*

We said our silent goodbyes before Dad held Mom's hand into the night. He was alone with her when she took her last troubled breath.

We buried Mom the next week. I hope and trust that she rests in peace.

There was no peace for me. Tortured by how poorly I had coped with her illness, I all but fled the scene.

It was back to Ak-Sar-Ben (Nebraska spelled backward) Race Track in Omaha, where I produced my first stakes winner. It was one of those never-to-be-forgotten moments, especially because it came astride a filly named Bye Bye Battle that I had helped to develop for J. J. Pletcher when she was a two-year-old. I had broken her for him—taught her to accept a rider and handle his instructions.

I was gratified that Bye Bye Battle had done well enough even to belong in a stakes race that had $25,000 added in purse money. Even though I knew nothing about her competition, I felt like I was meeting an old friend when we got reacquainted in the paddock. I had the utmost confidence in her, and she justified it by hustling to the lead and never looking back. My excitement level was unbelievable. I still remember receiving that check for $2,400. I looked hard at the figure, scarcely believing my eyes. I felt like a millionaire.

Hazel Park in Detroit was next, but it was not nearly as satisfying and proved to be a very short stay. It was brief because it appeared to me that more races were being fixed there than being run honestly.

My suspicions were aroused by a victory that was simply too easy. As I rode a particular race, I was flying by horses. I had done my handicapping and expected resistance from certain members of the field, but there was none. In fact, while I was whipping and driving, I looked around and saw the other jocks pulling on their horses as if it were a morning workout and they did not want their mounts to overdo it. It may not have been obvious to the casual fan, but it was obvious to me: These riders were doing their best to lose.

My concerns were confirmed an hour later when another rider approached me. "Little jock," he said, "if you want to stick around here, you've got to join the group."

I decided I would be neither a player nor a bystander. I left Detroit after two weeks.

I was approached to fix a race just one other time in my career, during my first year in Chicago in 1977. Again, the inquiry came from another jockey.

"Listen," he said, "you're riding a horse in the last race who looks like he has a good chance to win. Do you think you could get him beat without getting noticed?"

"No," I answered.

"You can't or you won't?"

"Won't."

End of discussion.

I've heard that plenty of games were played at small tracks in the 1940s and 1950s, when purse structures were terrible. Old-time trainers have told me they resorted to it because cashing a substantial bet was the only way they could pay their bills and leave town without being chased out.

As purse structures improved, the urgency to manipulate results eased. Frankly, the risk no longer justified the reward, since the more money that is bet on a specific horse, the lower the odds are driven.

I can say with certainty that it is virtually impossible to fix a marquee event such as the Kentucky Derby. With so many cameras rolling, any subtle action to slow a horse can be detected easily. Furthermore, no prominent trainer or jockey would think for a second about jeopardizing the millions of dollars in purse money involved.

AFTER MY BAD EXPERIENCE IN DETROIT, I WELCOMED the familiar ground of New Mexico and Santa Fe Downs. I was working with Chuck Sherman, my first real agent, and we were winning races hand over fist. It was unbelievable how well I was doing. Some of the horses did not look like much on form, but they were just marching.

> JIM: *Most of his races were pretty easy. He was just head and shoulders above the other riders. He had developed skills and could think out a race at seventeen.*

I probably would have been a match for my competitors even at equal weights, but with the five-pound allowance given to me as an apprentice, it was an unbeatable advantage. In 1975, I was the leading apprentice at Sunland Park and Ak-Sar-Ben, and one of the leading bug riders in the entire United States, with ninety-five victories and $298,848 in earnings.

Then the fun stopped. My mother's dying wish had been that I go to college. She thought I needed to advance my education beyond high school, and after mishandling her terminal illness so badly, I was not about to disagree.

I enrolled at the University of Texas at El Paso for the fall semester of 1975—only to quickly realize that I got along much better with Thoroughbreds than with professors, who could not possibly reach a young man whose mind was miles away. After two or three weeks, I was like a caged wild animal. I could not stay in the classroom. Time dragged as lecturers droned on. I know I made a halfhearted attempt, but I was so unhappy.

After my encouraging start as an apprentice, I could not help but believe that I was wasting my time and the time of those around me. I was also living at home and that did not help matters. It was awfully tame, awfully dull. A structured schedule and four walls, that was not a good fit for Jerry Bailey. My attendance became increasingly sporadic. I received an incomplete in every course—and that was it for me. I was a college man no longer.

I think Mom would be proud to know that I continue my education to this day, however. If I read a word I do not know, I look it up. If there is a point of business I do not understand, I ask an expert and make sure I grasp it. Although it depends on the individual, lack of a college degree was never a hindrance for me.

Most top riders have little more than a high school education, and for a very good reason. Their time is spent learning the lessons of the track rather than in the classroom.

Mom would not be proud to know, however, that I stepped up my partying as soon as I rejoined the racetrack scene. I had just turned eighteen. I was free and independent again, and I was making the most of it.

I was going out almost every night because that is what pretty much everybody around me did. We would order a couple of drinks, eat a light dinner, then drink some more. We never cared where the evening took us. Sometimes, it led to strange places.

There was the time I awoke with a jolt to the acrid smell of cleaning solvents. I could see in the darkness that I was crammed into a small space, with my knees pressed against my stomach.

There were sponges and soiled rags all around. Welcome to the mop closet at Caravan East, a nightclub in Albuquerque, New Mexico.

Somehow, I convinced myself there was nothing abnormal about this. I was eighteen. I had ample money to play with. I was playing—and playing hard!

That was not easy for those in my company. I was never a good drunk. I was like a little dog with a big bark. I could be belligerent and condescending. They say alcohol intensifies your personality, so I was very opinionated. It was as if the heavens above had given me, and only me, all the answers.

One of my scrapbooks contains a yellowed newspaper clipping with a headline that reads, "New Whiz Kid at the Track." I reveled in that. I believed every word of praise that was written. I was a big deal, and I bought a car befitting my stature from my uncle Harold's showroom.

My flashy ride gave new meaning to loud. Picture a fire-engine red Cadillac with a red-and-white-plaid interior. Uncle Harold charged me $8,200, which represented a $500 profit for him. I love my uncle, but he absolutely would not sell me that car at cost. The Baileys are all about business. Always.

My Cadillac featured every option except dice hanging from the rearview mirror. It was a scream for attention, and I got plenty of it. I thought back to Bobby Salas. He had nothing on me now or my new set of wheels.

I SET OUT FOR OAKLAWN PARK IN HOT SPRINGS, ARKANSAS, to begin the 1976 season. Bob Frieze was my agent and I was riding for Ray Spencer, a trainer I had known for a long time. Since purse money was poor, Ray was like many trainers: he would capitalize on inside knowledge to cash in on especially live starters.

There was nothing improper to any of this. Sometimes horses have sharp workouts that clockers simply do not see. Sometimes a change as basic as the way a horse is shod makes a dramatic difference. Sometimes a trainer finds the littlest thing wrong that he had not previously spotted and he knows that will make an improvement.

Under those kinds of circumstances, members of the barn tend to bet with both hands. For grooms, for instance, it is an important way to supplement an otherwise meager income. The fewer people in the know, the fatter the return.

Anyway, Ray confronted me halfway through the meet with a claim that Bob was giving out their secrets and killing prices on their horses. I never paid attention to the tote board. I was not an avid gambler then and am not now. If I bet twenty dollars on a race, that is plenty.

Ray insisted I change agents or lose his stable. To this day, I do not know if there was any validity to his charge. And even if it was true, Bob was doing nothing wrong—just costing Ray some of his winnings. I nonetheless dismissed Bob and hired Bill Shuman to be my agent. In a move I deeply regretted, I valued the chance to stay on live horses more than my relationship with Bob. That is typical of what a jockey will do in order to stay plugged into certain outfits.

While Bill was a really good guy and a decent agent, my association with him and his wife only accelerated my drinking. I would have dinner with them four or five times a week and liquor flowed like the mighty Mississippi.

I had stepped up from beer to vodka. Vodka tasted great. It seemed tame compared to the bite of scotch, but vodka is not tame. It is insidious. It creeps up on you like a thief in the night, and I never saw it approaching. I drank vodka and 7-Up, vodka and orange juice, vodka and damn near anything.

Veteran riders were not sure what to make of the "Whiz Kid." Due to my brief college stint, I had been granted an extension on my weight allowance and would be the leading apprentice at Oaklawn Park that season. But the combination of the flaming red Caddy, bell-bottoms, platform shoes, and shoulder-length blond hair made me quite a sight.

I remember waiting in the starting gate early in the Oaklawn meet and hearing John Lively call over to fellow veteran Larry Snyder, "Who's the girl on the four?"

"That's not a girl," Larry shouted. "That's the new bug rider."

Mom used to ask my dad, "What about his hair, Jim?"

"As long as it's clean and well put-together, it's okay," he would reply.

That was my dad. He did not have to agree with you as long as you handled things right. If we mishandled our affairs when we were kids, we received a painful reminder of his expectations. You bent over the bed and received three whacks from a wooden board. Dad did not take crap from anyone, especially his children.

I thought of my parents often in 1976, especially Mom. Instead of facing her death and coming to grips with it, I ran from it. I hardly ever called my father or my sisters. I detached from my family, anything associated with home. I did not want to deal with anyone who might make me remember Mom. It was torment enough that frequently I would think about her when I was alone in the middle of the night and start crying.

BECKY: *We didn't hear from him very often, for whatever reason. I guess he just needed time. Everybody deals with loss in his own way.*

My next stop was Chicago and an encounter with Ted Atkinson, a former jockey who was employed as a steward. I was expected to be extremely light for a certain mount that day and I alerted him that I would come in a couple of pounds overweight. That is usually not an issue of any kind. It was this time.

Atkinson looked the "Whiz Kid" up and down and said, "It looks like weight might be your problem, son. You might be just passing through."

I had never heard of Ted Atkinson. All I knew was that this guy was judging me without even knowing me, and it made me mad. Many youngsters stop being effective as soon as their weight allowance is gone, but the doubt he expressed just fueled my determination.

Although I lost my apprentice status before the Hawthorne meet, I became the leading rider—with thanks to Atkinson.

I also have fond memories of Hawthorne because it was there that I won my first turf race and fell in love with that part of the sport. I did not fall in love with Hawthorne's grass course. It was not pristine by any means, with little hills and valleys that made almost every stride an adventure.

I had been told that turf racing would require much more of me from a physical standpoint. In actuality, I was delighted with it because it demanded so much from me mentally, with its emphasis on patience and ground-saving. If you look at most riders, their physical attributes are pretty much the same. The mental aspect is what separates us. I was always confident that if I could not outride most of my rivals, I could outthink them.

Chicago was my kind of town for reasons that extended way beyond my success at Hawthorne. You can have just about anything you desire in the Windy City, and I was on a mission to prove that. Since I needed to pick up three years to meet the drinking age of twenty-one, a friend of a friend secured a driver's license that showed I was twenty-one. Access to clubs and booze, girls everywhere. Yeah, Chicago was my kind of town.

So was Miami. I tested the Florida circuit in 1976 and loved it. I will never forget the first time I laid eyes on the Atlantic Ocean. El Paso was almost desert like in its dryness. To suddenly gaze at water that stretched as far as I could see, not to mention the bikini-clad babes who filled the beaches, I knew what I had been missing through my teenage years.

I had just turned nineteen. There was ample time to make up for lost time. Girls and drinking, drinking and girls, those two pleasures were foremost on my mind. Riding, even though I represented Neal Winick's powerful barn, ran a distant third.

I would like to say my nightlife did not impact my sharpness in the morning, but that was not the case. My first couple of weeks in Florida, I never once made it to Calder Race Course to exercise the horses.

Neal's uncle, Arnold, had told me, "You don't have to come out if it's been raining. We don't do anything on muddy tracks." So each morning, I stumbled out of bed in my apartment, pulled the curtain back slightly to peek outside, saw that the lawns were wet, and went back to sleep.

This went on for a bit before Arnold finally asked, "Where the hell have you been?"

"What do you mean? You told me not to come out when it

rains. It's been raining every morning. Whenever I wake up, the ground is always soaked."

That is how I learned about water sprinklers—we did not have any in El Paso that I knew of—and why the grass is always green in Miami despite the scorching Florida sun.

I also came to understand the nuances of Calder's layout by studying races from a balcony. My room at the Holiday Inn was only some thirty yards removed from the far turn, with a head-on view down the backstretch, so it was a perfect vantage point. It is vital to a jockey's success to know how different tracks typically play. Is it a speed-favoring surface? Is the inside where you want to be? How should the turns be handled? While the answers to these questions can change on a given day, I still wanted to be aware of those tendencies going in.

I arrived in Florida with a secret weapon—my ability to speak Spanish fluently. I had studied the language from grammar school into high school and spoken it to Mexican workers my parents employed at our house. Since many riders in Florida are Hispanic and communicated in their native tongue even during races— shouting that they were making a move inside (*adentro*) or outside (*afuera*)—I allowed them to think I was in the dark whenever they spoke.

I maintained my silence for about three or four months until one day a Puerto Rican rider entered the jocks' room and was rattling off insults at the *rubia* (blond). I fired back at him in perfect Spanish. The bewildered expressions on the faces of the Hispanic members of the jockey colony—the realization that they had been had—was worth giving up my edge.

Speaking of looking for an edge, I've never met anyone so bent on finding an angle as Jimmy the Greek. I met the handicapper and self-proclaimed gambling expert soon after I began competing in Florida. We met in the paddock one day and a cordial relationship developed. He started calling my house, always with the same question:

"Do you like anything today?"

As I mentioned earlier, I am a terrible handicapper. I am skilled at assessing how contenders will be positioned with a quarter of a mile to go and where my horse must be placed to have his best possible chance. From that point on, don't ask me.

Jimmy the Greek did ask me and I did my best to answer, much to the amusement of my best friend and roommate, Bryan Fann. One day the Greek called with his usual question.

"Do you like anything today?"

"Well, I'm on six horses and the only one I like is in the stakes race. He's the lone speed in the race. I'm pretty sure I can make the lead and keep on going."

When I returned home, Bryan asked me how I did. "You're not going to believe this," I told him. "I won five races. I won every race—except the stakes race."

Bryan loved it. "At least the Greek won't be calling here anymore," he said.

The phone rang the next morning.

"Do you like anything today?"

Even if I could never anticipate my success, in 1977 I began making a name for myself at Gulfstream Park, a major track in Hallandale Beach, Florida. I won $100,000 stakes races on four successive Saturdays there: the Canadian Turf Handicap, the Seminole, the Gulfstream Park Handicap and the Pan American Handicap.

The fifth Saturday nearly brought disaster. I was approached by a trainer I did not know well and asked if I could work a horse for him because the owner was coming to watch. Foolishly, I obliged—and my unscheduled mount bolted, crashed into another horse, and I fell. The other horse, understandably, panicked and stepped on my jaw. It broke in two places.

The only positive aspect of my first major injury was that it reconnected me with my family, albeit briefly. Becky, a registered nurse, flew to get me. My father made sure I received the best care while I recovered at home.

I needed to prepare all of my food in a blender. I had lost a tooth in the accident, and that made a convenient opening for a straw. I would combine bacon and oatmeal for breakfast. I even put a steak through the blender once, just to enjoy the taste of red meat again.

The broken jaw did nothing to slow the pace of my drinking, however. Actually, since I had no responsibilities, it increased. With so little in my stomach, two drinks were enough to send me into the drunken stupor that was such a pleasurable escape for me. I kept a pair of wire cutters at my side in case I felt nauseous and needed to vomit. Fortunately, they remained at my side.

It was almost three months before I was cleared to return to work. The collision and its consequences never made me fearful. What stuck in my mind was that I would never again accept a horse I was not scheduled to work. I became a lot more cautious about whose stock I would be willing to breeze.

I later discovered that that horse had bolted before. A repeat might have been unavoidable. It sure would have helped if I had been forewarned. It is a trainer's responsibility to prepare the rider for any issues that might arise. I was failed badly in that regard, and my jaw paid the price.

I kept my stay at home as brief as possible. My family was there when I needed them. As soon as they could no longer help me, I wanted to be elsewhere. My communication with my father and sisters went back to being an infrequent phone call—and they were always the ones who called.

I flew to California with my jaw still wired shut to prepare for my return to competition. This may sound insignificant to the casual fan, but the most important thing that happened to me during my first venture to the West Coast was when I walked into the locker room and Bill Shoemaker turned to me and said, "Hey, Jerry, how are you doing?"

Bill Shoemaker had heard of me! He knew my name! The best jockey in the world knew my name!

I was even more flattered when he put a hot spoon to the back of my elbow. Let me explain.

Shoe typically walked around the locker room with a cup of coffee and a spoon he used to stir it. He was always a prankster, and one of his favorite pranks was to touch an unsuspecting victim with that hot spoon. To be spooned by Shoe, there could be no higher honor. That meant you were part of the group.

Sometimes Shoe's humor was more subtle. He was playing cards one day when the masseur approached to tell him his wife, Babs, was calling. Shoe looked up from his hand.

"Tell her I'm in the box," he said.

We all broke up. The ninety-five-pound Shoe never needed the help of the hot box to control his weight. But the masseur dutifully relayed that message to Babs. Shoe and his wife used to argue off and on, and I guess the fight must have been "on" that day.

Other than my immediate acceptance by Shoe, which meant more to me than words can convey, my first experience at Hollywood Park in Inglewood, California, was noteworthy for only one race. It is so important that a rider have a reputation for courage. I made a name for myself that way strictly by accident.

I was handling a live long shot, Dreaming of Moe, in a $40,000 stake at Hollywood. He was within striking distance and pulling on me hard as we approached the turn for home. It finally got to the point that he was unrestrainable. He wanted to go. He wanted to go now. I searched for a crease between horses and finally found one.

If I had my choice, I would never have tried to split those horses. Dreaming of Moe decided for me. He was making his move, whether I was ready or not. The maneuver, an attempt at survival because he was prepared to run over one of the horses blocking us if he had to, was hardly silky-smooth. We caused some bumping, probably some hard feelings, too, but not enough to be disqualified. We split those horses and won. I was praised in the papers the next morning for my daring. Ignorance is bliss sometimes.

Otherwise, the West Coast and I were not a good fit. I had no friends there, not even friends of friends who might slip me into nightclubs. At twenty, I was still a year below the drinking age.

I tried to make the best of things. I won a few races and had some fun. I lived in posh Marina Del Rey. I appeared as an extra on a Hollywood set. In truth, though, I was someone trying to find his way, and not doing a very good job of it.

My life would be aimless until I regained my sobriety in January 1989. I was doing well enough, making good enough money, but I could not touch the top riders on their best day.

Sadly, that was fine with me. I had grown up idolizing Bart Starr. I wanted to throw deep for the Green Bay Packers, just the way Bart did. When I'd found out that was not to be, there were times when I simply did not care what happened. And that included racing.

The minimal effort I gave to my career was particularly obvious when I rode at New Jersey's Monmouth Park in the summer in the late 1970s.

BRYAN: *We called him the "two-o'clock jock" because he rode so many late races that he didn't have to be in the jocks' room until two o'clock.*

He was a good rider. You couldn't really understand why he wasn't busier. He kind of floated along. He had one or two a day. He was pretty content with that.

My unflattering nickname should have embarrassed me into doing something about it. Two-o'clock jock? I laughed along with everyone else.

When I was with Bryan, we were always looking to crack up the room. Monmouth Park supplies a swimming pool for exercise and relaxation. One of the unwritten rules is that someone, anyone, is subject to being thrown into the pool if he appears on the deck wearing anything other than a bathing suit.

One afternoon, I spotted Bryan in racing silks as he approached my lounge chair. Immediately, I was plotting his wet demise. He said something I could not hear. I signaled him to come closer. When he did, I leaped up, grabbed him, and hurled him into the pool.

As I was doing so, the thought crossed my mind that something was very wrong with the picture. This was like the odds-on horse who looks too good to be true. This heave-ho was too easy.

As Bryan plunged headfirst into the pool, my fears were realized. I saw "Bailey" stitched on the back of his pants. Worse still, when he climbed out, I saw that my custom-made boots—black, with cherry-red tops—had gone the way of the pants. I tried to salvage them by putting them in the sun to dry. They shrank. Laughter filled the room as it became obvious I would never force those boots onto my feet again.

Another time, word came down to the jocks' room that no one was to wear bikini underwear to the pool. The administrative offices overlook the water. Some secretaries thought we should cover up a bit more. Bryan and I donned traditional swimsuits and said we wanted to make sure the offended staffers were satisfied. When they looked down at us, nods of approval quickly turned to shock. We had cut out the backs of our bathing suits. As we turned around, we mooned our disapproval.

Two-o'clock jock? I am embarrassed by that now. I hate the fact that the moniker once applied. How could that have been?

I think alcohol dims your perspective and harms your self-esteem. Sure, I was familiar with the Kentucky Derby and made sure to watch it every year on television. In the early years of my career, I never thought I would be good enough to ride in one. I was not even motivated to be part of the action on the first Saturday in May.

My priorities were elsewhere. Dating Stacey Winick, now that was a priority. Old Arnold had warned me to stay away from his daughter if I wanted to keep working for him. Of course, that only drove me to see her all the more, and I lost the stable over it.

Instead of being repentant, I continued dating Stacey a year after Arnold found out. I liked Stacey. I liked sticking it to Arnold just as much.

I was not looking for a long-term relationship with Stacey or any of the women I met at that time. I was living in the moment. I was lusting after immediate satisfaction with the most attractive women I could hook, nothing more. Finding someone to share my life was the last thought on my mind. It was as important for me to take care of business at night as it was in the morning.

That reputation was starting to precede me. When I approached Doc Danner about being my agent for the meet at Keeneland Race Course in Lexington, Kentucky, in 1982, he was hesitant.

"I heard you won't work in the morning," he said, "and you'll try to steal my girlfriend."

"No, no, no," I insisted. "I will be there at five o'clock every morning and you don't have to worry about your girl. What kind of guy do you think I am, anyway?"

This was one vow I kept. I was among Keeneland's leading riders and topped the list in purses earned. As for Doc's girlfriend, I stayed away as promised. She still wound up with another man. Love on the backstretch can be a fleeting feeling.

I am indebted to Doc for lining up my initial Derby shot, a horse named New Discovery. It was unforgettable to reach the main track at Churchill Downs and hear them play "My Old Kentucky Home" for the first time. I felt goose bumps, just like they said I would. That peculiar tingle continues to run up and down my body before every Derby, even now.

Although my mount was lightly regarded, I entered the Derby

with my buttons popping a little bit. Just the race before I had won the $50,000 Twin Spires Stakes for the same owner, Eugene Jacobs, aboard Cutaway. We'd stalked the leaders and he'd drawn off with mild urging, justifying my confidence in him.

I had worked both Cutaway and New Discovery many times and always told Mr. Jacobs that I thought Cutaway was the better horse by far. He'd chosen New Discovery for the Derby because he thought he was better equipped to handle the mile and a quarter.

Given how well Cutaway performed, and the fact that in the Derby, New Discovery dropped back steadily and finished eighteenth of nineteen, that decision proved to be a second-guesser's delight.

As for me, though, I did not really give the outcome a second thought. My attention was on driving from Louisville to Lexington so I could catch a flight to New York. I had one hour and forty-five minutes to do so. Exactly an hour after the Derby, I reached Lexington. That is how quickly I was moving. That is how quickly I put my first Run for the Roses behind me.

I have never been one to dwell on what-ifs. That is nothing but wasted energy. Whatever has happened, happened. I cannot do anything to change it. I can do something about the next day's racing card—provided I get there.

Cutaway, incidentally, continued to justify my belief that he belonged in Triple Crown races by running a solid third in the Preakness. New Discovery turned out to be just another one of those horses who participated in the Derby but did not really belong there.

The timing was right when John Dale, an agent, called and asked me about riding in New York. He would handle my book there. John was a good man, a funny man who never intended to be that way.

A spinal condition had caused his head to be permanently tilted. There is not a lot of political correctness at the track, so John was widely referred to as "Ten to two."

Apparently, everybody knew this except "Señor" Luro, who had a similar affliction.

The first time John approached Luro and asked, "Do you have any horses for Jerry?" the trainer just glared.

"Funny man," he said at last.

It took some time before I explained the situation to both of them and cooled that down.

I went to New York on a two-week trial and did not win a race there. I decided to stay anyway. I was not intimidated by the setting at all, although mid-Manhattan traffic was another story. I cracked the top ten in a very strong jockey colony.

John and I did well enough together for the next couple of years and I am indebted to him for booking me on Fit to Fight, who was trained by Mack Miller and owned by powerful Rokeby Stable.

In 1984, Fit to Fight swept New York's Triple Crown for handicap horses—the Metropolitan, Suburban and Brooklyn handicaps. Our journey in the Metropolitan alone helped establish my reputation in the hugely demanding New York market.

Although we faced a field of fourteen that day, I knew there was only one horse to fear. That was A Phenomenon, a heavy favorite due to his high early speed and because he would be handled by Angel Cordero, Jr. Angel was as good as it got at that time.

My ideal scenario was to sit third or fourth in the early stages, several lengths off the lead. Angel, who was no angel, would not have that. He did his damnedest to pin me down on the rail, one of his favorite ploys.

A jockey's typical response to that is to use more of his horse to prompt the pace. The faster the fractions, the more the starters get strung out, and the easier it is to pass. Compare it to highway driving. Is it easier to pass someone in a reduced-speed construction zone or when you are cruising at sixty-five miles per hour?

My change in strategy worked perfectly. By the time we reached the turn, Fit to Fight enjoyed outside position on A Phenomenon. My challenge was just beginning. Which rider could get home first? Angel was one of the strongest jockeys in the country, if not the strongest. Matching him would not be enough. I needed to beat him.

With whips flying, Fit to Fight was head to head with A Phenomenon. We asked for whatever was left. Still nose to nose. Then, at the end, we pushed ahead ever so slightly. Fit to Fight won that war by a head. I showed Mack and Rokeby Stable that I could slug it out with Angel Cordero, Jr., and not flinch.

WHILE I EXPECTED THAT JOHN DALE AND I WOULD have long-term success, change is often in the wind at the racetrack. That wind generally kicks up when you least expect it. Such was the case when I came upon Bob Frieze, my former agent, and learned he had been fired that day by Eddie Maple.

"What are you going to do?" he asked me.

"What do you mean, 'What am I going to do?'"

He explained to me that Maple had just hired John to represent him.

I felt betrayed.

"Give me a couple of days," I told Bob, "and I'll call you back."

I immediately phoned Lenny Goodman, a well-respected agent who was recuperating from major heart surgery. He was not ready to return to work yet. He arranged for another agent to handle my affairs for the next few weeks until he could resume his normal activities. If I did not already understand it, I was about to be given a firsthand lesson in the importance of a good agent.

My business went down the tubes in ten days. That agent had me jumping off horses with whom I had already done well to get on bad ones. He misled owners and trainers. He offended just about everyone he dealt with.

I could not wait another day. I called Bob Frieze with one instruction. "Go to work."

He went to work for me from 1984 until 2000 and really did a heck of a job. I needed an agent who would be a stabilizing influence in my life and he was that. Bob was a good family man with four daughters, and, yes, I stayed away from his daughters.

While some agents are no better than thieves, Bob showed there is honor among thieves. Doing the right thing was as important to him as getting me on the horse that looked best on paper. He believed in loyalty and nothing more complicated than doing the right thing.

While I already subscribed to these qualities, Bob reinforced them. He developed a trusting relationship with trainers and owners that allowed me not only to retain my core business but to dramatically expand on it.

The jockey-agent relationship can best be explained this way. If you see a successful jockey, rest assured he has a hardworking, quality agent behind him. A good agent is worth every bit of the twenty-five percent we pay them. A bad one, who does not build relationships and whose word is meaningless, can be all but ruinous.

There were times when I disappointed Bob and made his job much harder than it had to be. I always showed up for work. It was just that there was no telling how hungover I might be when I arrived.

There was a time in 1983 when Luro wanted me to breeze Tap Shoes six furlongs at Hialeah in Florida. Bryan was staying with me at the time and we drank well into the night. I asked Bryan to make sure I woke up in time to work Tap Shoes, an important mount, at 5:30 A.M. He did that and later met me at Hialeah.

"How did the horse work?" Bryan asked.

"He worked great, just the way Señor Luro wanted him to go," I answered.

"I'm sure he was impressed with you," Bryan continued.

"What do you mean?"

"First of all, your eyes are all bloodshot. Second, you're wearing your jacket inside out."

Sure enough, I had somehow pulled on my jacket with the lining facing out.

We doubled over with laughter. We laughed until we cried.

Four
_____

TIME FOR A CHANGE

I looked into the crowd and saw one person.

It was the spring of 1984 and love—or at least intense attraction—was in the air at Hialeah Park in Florida. I was preparing to ride Time for a Change in the Flamingo Stakes, which at the time was a key race for promising three-year-olds, when I spotted Suzee Chulick. She was a reporter for the New York–based SportsChannel, and she was wending her way through the stands with a camera crew behind her.

I had no inkling she would be the person who would change my life. All I saw was a blonde-haired beauty with a figure to match. I was not going to allow her to pass by.

I leaned over to Bryan Fann, my best friend then and now. "I'm going to ask that girl out," I told him.

I knew she would need to interview the winning jockey, so I rode in the Flamingo as if my life depended on it—which, in hindsight, perhaps it did.

Time for a Change responded with the race of his career, which he had to, given the quality of the competition. Devil's Bag and Dr. Carter were likely to be the chief opposition. Devil's Bag was all the rage but untested to this point. He possessed early speed in abundance (as did Time for a Change). Dr. Carter, I knew, would save his best for late.

After studying the past performances, I saw only one way to beat Devil's Bag, who would start outside with Dr. Carter to the inside. Time for a Change would have to grab the overwhelming favorite by the throat and never let go. As for Dr. Carter, I would have to rely on my horse's courage to fend him off after a speed duel.

The opening of the Flamingo started with the expected— Eddie Maple wanted the lead with Devil's Bag, all right—but to my surprise, Jorge Velasquez also sent Dr. Carter. I was part of the fray as well.

Devil's Bag had really exploded out of the gate, and Maple was starting to draw clear of us and ease over toward the rail. I sensed a moment of indecision in Velasquez and then he backed Dr. Carter off. My mission was as clear to me now as it had been when I studied the *Daily Racing Form*.

We attacked.

When Devil's Bag accelerated up the backside, Time for a Change was pressing, pressing, pressing. When Maple looked to give Devil's Bag a breather, we would not allow it. We were at the leader's throat from the half-mile to the quarter-mile pole.

They say you do not truly know about a horse, do not truly

know if he bears the heart of a champion, until a rival looks him in the eye.

Time for a Change glared. Devil's Bag blinked.

We turned for home and Time for a Change was still throwing haymakers. Maple struck Devil's Bag once. No response. Again, Maple lifted his stick high and brought it down with all the force he could muster. Devil's Bag was shortening his stride.

As soon as I knew we had exposed the ballyhooed Devil's Bag, along came Dr. Carter. Having sat off the punishing fractions, he was now full of run. I can still hear his heavy breathing as he ranged up outside.

Time for the last part of my plan. Because I knew my horse had a penchant for lugging in, I switched the whip to my left hand and went to work with the stick while pushing on his neck with my right hand. Time for a Change sped across the finish line with his head in front.

Time to claim my reward! Suzee did indeed come over to interview me, and after I answered her questions and talked excitedly about Time for a Change as my Derby horse, she said she needed additional footage. That was the opening I'd been waiting for. I returned to the jocks' room holding aloft a scrap of paper with a phone number as if it were the Flamingo trophy itself.

"I just met this nice girl from New York," I told Bryan.

BRYAN: *If anybody else was riding that horse that day, he doesn't win. When he came back to the jocks' room, I said, "J.D., let me tell you something. You never rode a race better than that one."*

When he got into the stretch, he never missed a beat. He was on the fence and he was hitting him right-handed, then left-handed. He never let up. He was like a machine on that horse.

SUZEE: *I had made a pact with myself never to date athletes I inter-*
viewed. There were not many female sports reporters in the early
eighties. I knew there were certain lines that should not be crossed—
for my sake and for those who would follow in my footsteps.

But Jerry was so kind to me during our interview. He could see I
was new to the sport and he helped me through. And his eyes drew
me to him. They are beautiful and blue. I felt there was so much
behind them.

It was a scary feeling, like nothing I had ever experienced before
or since. I wasn't ready for that feeling yet. I thought to myself,
"My gosh, something might change here."

Although an injury kept Time for a Change from going on to
the Derby, all was not lost. When I returned to competition in
New York, one of the first things I did was to dig out that scrap of
paper. Suzee was on my mind constantly. I could not wait to get
to know her.

Every time I called, though, I reached a switchboard for some
hotel. I tried to contact her at different hours of the day and
night. She never answered. I had no way of knowing that a mod-
eling agency had arranged for her to live at the Hotel Tudor in
New York City. Not surprisingly, Suzee saved the situation, as she
would on a much larger scale later on.

She came to the track and spotted my agent, John Dale.

"Jerry's been trying to reach you," John told her, "but he keeps
getting this hotel."

She cleared up the confusion and I broke one of my rules to
arrange our first date. Because driving in Manhattan is nothing
like tooling around El Paso or motoring anywhere else in the civ-

ilized world, I had vowed not to date anyone who lived outside a five-mile radius from my place in Queens. But I literally went the extra mile—make that miles—for Suzee. I braved traffic that intimidated me the way a cluster of horses never did.

I took her to the Pen & Pencil, a traditional steakhouse, for our first date. There was none of the initial awkwardness that can make conversation so uncomfortable. She grew up in Benld, Illinois, which has a population of fifteen hundred or so, and she shared my passion for sports, having lettered in volleyball, track, softball and bowling during high school, where she'd been one of approximately 120 students in her graduating class.

She told me about her budding career, which had taken her in several different directions after she attended the University of Missouri School of Journalism. She had appeared in commercials for Diet Sprite, Ford Mustang and Speedy Muffler while auditioning for roles in films.

As she conveyed to me what an out-of-control, cocaine-filled world Hollywood could be, she emphasized that she was anchored to values that would never allow her to be swept up in that whirl. She had served as a lector in her church, she had brought warmth and sustenance to the homeless through work in soup kitchens. There was more to Suzee than to any woman I had ever met before. As I enjoyed my meal and paced myself with scotch and water, I only hoped that she was as drawn to me as I was to her.

SUZEE: *There was a spark of unpredictability in him that I liked. He had a little bit of a wild animal in him that I thought I could tame.*

I regularly sent flowers to Suzee, and did everything else I could think of to let her know this was more than a casual relationship to me. My attraction to her went far beyond physical beauty. She was caring and affectionate, and her loving touch was something I badly needed.

I wanted to be there for her, as well, and the need arose when her grandfather, John, died a few months into our relationship. I flew to Illinois and met her parents, Fran and Jack.

Fran was immediately wary of me because she cooked huge meals and I politely turned away most of what she served. Of course, it had nothing to do with the quality of the food, which was excellent, and everything to do with the need to keep my weight under control. So many jockeys have eaten their way out of a career, and I was not about to be one of them.

Beyond the fact that I could not eat heartily, I could tell there was something else about me that bothered Suzee's mother.

FRAN: *He seemed like a real gentleman, but I remembered reading stories in the newspaper about racing and the fast crowd it attracted. I have to admit I was a bit apprehensive.*

Things went better with Jack. He was a dentist, like my father, so at least that gave us a starting point for discussion. I thought it only proper to take him aside and let him know how serious I was about his daughter. I asked for his blessing if we were to become engaged, and he assured me he wanted whatever was best for Suzee.

JACK: *He seemed like a respectful young man and I liked him. But I was a bit taken aback by how fast their relationship was moving, especially when marriage was mentioned.*

Summer was quickly upon us. That meant the annual meet at Saratoga Race Course in Saratoga Springs, New York. It's a gorgeous track and a much-anticipated time of year on the New York racing calendar, and the track and the town pack them in. I invited Suzee to share the house I was renting. I was determined to show her and anyone else paying attention that I was ready to dethrone the reigning King of Saratoga, Angel Cordero, Jr.

But—not exactly.

In my very first race, my mount, Will of Iron, stumbled leaving the gate, and I tumbled head over heels to the track, breaking my collarbone. Suzee received the kind of call I had hoped to spare her, at least in the early years of our relationship.

SUZEE: *The reality hit me, "This is what this guy does. This kind of injury, or worse, can happen every time he gets on a horse." As upset as I was about what had happened, I knew I had to be there for him.*

I was bitterly disappointed. My time to shine instead turned to too much idle time. I took medication to handle my physical discomfort. Alcohol dulled my emotional distress. The more Suzee reminded me that painkillers and alcohol do not mix, the more I combined them.

I drank when she was with me and tried to push as many cocktails on her as possible. I already had Bryan matching me shot for shot. I saw no reason why she should not do the same. There is a reason why alcoholics do not socialize with nondrinkers for very long. I felt more at ease when those around me held full glasses.

Suzee excused my consumption while we were in Saratoga, saying she knew how upset I was about being sidelined. As a for-

mer athlete, she could understand how much I missed competition. I quickly agreed.

We decided we both needed a change of scenery and made the
short trip to Lake Placid, New York, a place where couples have
long gone in search of romance. That did not keep me from
drinking throughout our stay. Did that have anything to do with
what happened next? It's hard to say.

At the start of dinner one evening, I asked Suzee the question
that had been on my mind almost from the instant I'd spotted her
in the Hialeah crowd.

"Will you marry me?"

"Wow," she said, grasping the seriousness of a question I asked
almost casually. Then came the answer I was waiting for.

"Yes."

I allowed a few minutes to go by before I asked a second question that was almost as important to me as the first—and that's
when I blew it.

"Will you sign a prenuptial agreement?"

Truth be told, I was far from wealthy then. But that is not how
I perceived myself. I was paranoid. I always thought other people
were pursuing assets that I had risked my life daily to obtain. If I'd
been worth as much as I thought I was, I would never have had to
ride again. That is how important I thought I was.

But Suzee soon popped that bubble. She did not have to think
long about this answer, either. She stormed out.

When we returned to Saratoga the next day, she stayed just
long enough to pack her belongings.

"You can't leave me like this," I said, pleading my broken collarbone. I would use anything to gain her sympathy. Or try to.

"We're through," she shot back, and she returned to New York City to live with her girlfriends.

SUZEE: *I prayed a lot and cried a lot. I worked to get my career back on track. In a business that is all about seizing opportunities, I had already missed so many of them to spend time with Jerry and cater to his needs.*

I remember getting a callback for a commercial for Taco Bell. As much as I tried to focus on convincing them I was the face and voice they needed to sell tacos, I broke down during the audition. I had opened up myself emotionally. I was hurt and frightened and lost.

I had no idea what Suzee was going through. I was twenty-seven going on seventeen. They say that sometime between eighteen and twenty-five you quit partying and become a responsible, mature adult. That happened long after twenty-five for me.

When Suzee would verbalize her feelings, I listened. But I did not understand. When she expressed concern that her career might be passing her by, I could not grasp what she was worried about. I knew I could provide well for her and our family. Why not just drop everything and come along for the fun?

I did not have the capacity to think or care about anybody but myself. My philosophy was that I had always taken care of myself from a young age, so I was not responsible for taking care of her and her emotional needs. Most of the time, I showed little outward emotion and was as restrained as my parents.

Although Suzee asked me not to call, I did not listen. I phoned her repeatedly and leaned on her friends to coax her to the phone. They always insisted she was not home. I later discovered she had resumed dating someone she had been seeing prior to our relationship.

SUZEE: *I prayed so much during our separation. I prayed to the Virgin Mary. I prayed to his mother, Betty, even though I had never met her. "Please help your son. Please help your son."*

Summer passed into autumn and autumn to winter before I finally persuaded Suzee to give me another chance. She joined me in Florida, not knowing what to expect. I proposed again, this time with a ring in hand that I had purchased through a family friend in El Paso. Maybe that prenuptial agreement was not so important after all.

She accepted—and this time there was no second question.

The next order of business was setting a date. We visited a church in Great Neck, Long Island, and told the monsignor of our intentions. He regretted to inform us that the church was heavily booked. We would have to wait two years for the next opening.

"On a Tuesday?" I blurted.

I explained to him the wedding had to be on a Tuesday because there was no New York racing that day. I would not have to miss any mounts. Neither would my colleagues at the track.

Tuesdays, he assured me, would not be a problem. We selected December 17, 1985.

Then he asked for our addresses. We gave him mine.

The monsignor shook his head in disapproval. "Do you know you are living in sin?"

We told him we were aware of that. We explained about an issue with Suzee's lease. She would have been obligated to pay for the space she was renting long after we were married. With significant expenses ahead of us, that made no sense.

"Well," the monsignor replied, "you will have to give me different addresses because I cannot send this into the bishop." We appreciated his understanding and got through the paperwork.

Meanwhile, another problem was developing that could not be so easily solved. Simply put, my father and Suzee did not mix. He was convinced she had gold on her mind and dollar signs in her heart. Frankly, he was rude to her from the start.

I always delighted in the attractiveness of my fiancée. The first time I introduced my father to her, I held out my hand in Suzee's direction and said, "Isn't she the most beautiful woman you ever saw?"

Dad looked her up and down. "She's all right," he muttered.

Suzee, hurt though she was, tried to make light of the matter by referring to her "ski-jump nose."

"Looks like you broke it a few times," Dad said.

That was enough. I was furious and admonished my father in front of the rest of the family. "I love this girl," I told him. "If you don't treat her well, you can say goodbye to both of us." To this day, I do not know what Dad was thinking about, how he could have been so hurtful to someone preparing to join our family.

BECKY: *To my father, my mother was the most beautiful woman he'd ever seen. He's just very direct. It's just my dad. He is not going to say something he doesn't feel.*

JIM: *I sure as hell could have been more diplomatic and wish I had been. At the time, I wasn't. I may have been a burr in her saddle all along.*

Suzee's mother was not so sure of me, either. When she and Jack helped their daughter move in with me that summer, she found booze bottles in desk drawers, booze bottles in closets, booze bottles damn near everywhere.

FRAN: *I was happy for my daughter because I knew how important family was and is to her. I knew she always wanted a big family. But I was worried that she might be blinded by emotion.*

She had worked so hard to make it in New York and finally seemed to be doing very well for herself. I had hoped she wouldn't just throw it all away, especially on a young man who seemed to have demons lurking deep inside. I was raised in a bar-restaurant and had seen firsthand the terrible effect alcohol has on some people. I was reminded of those people whenever I saw Jerry drink.

Was I worried? Absolutely. Could I do anything about it? Not really. Suzee is very much like Jerry in that once she sets her mind on something, there is no holding her back.

SUZEE: *I was alarmed and embarrassed. I did what I could to cover up the situation. I told them Jerry regularly invited friends over. The bottles must belong to them. I told them I was sure Jerry had cut back on his drinking. My parents respected my wishes. They contin- ued unpacking my belongings—and worrying that their daughter was making a terrible mistake.*

I am sure their concerns only deepened the day I rode a horse named Charging Falls for Jack Van Berg in the Fall Highweight Handicap at Belmont Park. I was tracking First Guess, a front-runner ridden by Robbie Davis who started to drift out slightly. I knew that would create an opening for another contender to push up the rail, and I didn't want that. I angled my horse in and chirped to him, until I was shoulder to shoulder with Robbie, keeping him from drifting and slamming the door on anyone at the rail.

Just as I was congratulating myself on the maneuver, I heard a loud snap, the kind of sound you'd hear if you broke a tree branch over your leg to use for kindling. First Guess had shattered his leg. He would have to be humanely destroyed, but even worse for me, he wiped out my mount as he went down. I flew through the air and struck the ground hard. I knew there were flying hooves behind me. My only chance, perhaps for survival, was to roll away from the rail toward the center of the track. I rolled and rolled. It seemed that I rolled for thirty minutes. When would I be clear of the field?

The jarring answer came in the form of a huge blow to my back. Laffit Pincay had been trying to steer Pancho Villa toward the center of the track. I had rolled directly into his path.

Immediately, I fought to breathe. Every time I took in air, the pain was excruciating. I waited for help and demanded answers to questions that can never be answered.

"Why me?"

"Why again?"

It had been only little more than a year since I had fallen victim to Will of Iron's stumble. Although my latest accident would leave me with broken vertebrae, three broken ribs and a fractured left foot, time and the grim sight through the years of motionless counterparts would help me understand how fortunate I was.

At least I was alive. At least I could move my arms and legs.

Despite the setback, I approached my bachelor party in Floral Park, New York, in high spirits. It may have been an event to remember—if only I could remember it.

I went in with the attitude that this was one time when you are allowed to do anything you want. I came out of it completely wasted. My friends thought I was a cheap drunk. The truth is, that evening, like so many before and after it, I had already consumed several drinks before I arrived at the party. I was already buzzing. I only needed a couple more shots to put me over the top—and I went far beyond a couple more.

Ask me to run down the guest list. I cannot. Ask me what I said and did on what should have been one of the most cherished nights of my life. Not happening.

In actuality, it was just another night of excess, not to mention an angry exchange with Suzee's father when he tried to persuade me to turn over my car keys to him.

I began a perilous drive home made more so by my inability to find my exit. I tried this turn and that. Each time, the exit emptied into an unfamiliar neighborhood.

Finally, Suzee's father had seen enough.

JACK: *He was making a fool of himself. He was totally inebriated. I asked his father to stop him. Jim said he and Jerry had gone a long time without speaking following a disagreement. He didn't want that to happen again. He didn't want any part of this dispute. He sat silent.*

My son Jack and I told Jerry to get the heck out of the car. We were mad and we weren't going to keep going with him behind the wheel. He finally pulled over in front of Shea Stadium and Jack drove us home from there.

Suzee's parents and my friends were still angry at me the next day for wanting to drive when I absolutely should not have been driving. Their concerns extended beyond me. There is no telling how many innocent people I could have killed in that condition. All I could do was admit that they were right and I was wrong.

My alcoholism had progressed so far that my misadventures behind the wheel never once led me to think I should stop. I decided I had consumed far too much alcohol that night, more than ever before. I made a silent vow not to drink to that extent again.

As for Suzee, I can only imagine what she must have been thinking. In retrospect, I am amazed she went through with the wedding, understanding now how fragile she felt. Only a week before we were married, she had upset her agents by turning down a lucrative opportunity to become a news broadcaster in Boston, because the television station would have required her to live there.

Given the way I had been acting, was I someone she should give up her career for? If our marriage did not work out, what would happen to her then?

While my fiancée agonized, I drank heavily with my family immediately following the wedding rehearsal.

SUZEE: *I remember that Don MacBeth, a jockey who was a good friend of Jerry's, came up to my dad and said, "Your daughter has her work cut out for her." Another person said, "If this marriage makes it, it's going to be a miracle."*

As late as the morning of the wedding, I did not know if I wanted to go through with it.

I knew that I dared not embarrass myself or Suzee on our wedding day. I made it a point not to drink. I had the decency to know this was the most important day of our lives. I could not trust myself to have one or two. It helped that I never liked the taste of champagne.

Our wedding reception was everything we had hoped it would be. There had been tensions between the two families. For this day at least, the Baileys and the Chulicks understood the sanctity of the moment and shared in our joy. Suzee's grandmother, Mary, set the tone. She was ninety. She danced as if she were ready to high-step for another ninety.

Our honeymoon did not go nearly as well. We chose Aruba because it hardly ever rains there. We endured a bumpy landing in a downpour.

The weather did not matter to me, anyway. I spent half the vacation either going out to buy liquor or drinking. A honeymoon is just another word for vacation, isn't it? I was going to do what I damn well pleased.

SUZEE: *We got to Aruba and he started drinking heavily. He was Dr. Jekyll and Mr. Hyde. The monster was starting to come out. We spent wonderful days together on Aruba. The nights were awful. I felt so alone on my honeymoon. When we were together, the smell of alcohol repulsed me. I felt I was lying beside a person I did not even know.*

I had a great time in Aruba. We left there still married. I considered my honeymoon a success.

Five

OUT OF CONTROL

*F*ailure, by anyone's measure, came two years later.
"You're fired!"

Trainer Mack Miller never used those words when he met
with me in the autumn of 1986 because he was too much of a
gentleman for that, too much of a friend. But he slowly worked
his way around to that point.

I was stunned. Shouldn't have been, but was.

I would no longer be getting a leg up from Mack? Wouldn't
be riding all those well-bred horses sent to him by Paul Mellon?

Recently, we'd had two disqualifications in major stakes races
in New Jersey, and I knew we were all frustrated by that. It is difficult enough to breed, train and ride a horse so that he blossoms
into a winner, but then to cross the finish line ahead of the field

and be denied the first-place purse because the stewards detected a foul—there is nothing more exasperating.

In each instance, I had not reacted swiftly enough. At Monmouth Park, I'd been aboard Danger's Hour when he began tiring and lugging in. When that happens, a jockey must immediately begin whipping with his left hand to straighten out his mount, but because I was a split second slow to switch the stick to my left hand, we made brief contact with another horse. I didn't think circumstances warranted a change in the order of finish, but obviously the stewards disagreed.

The second time was much worse. My repeated left-handed urging in a $150,000 turf stakes at the Meadowlands had caused my mount to impede a horse named Fred Astaire. I have no defense for it. It wasn't because I was drunk. I was never drunk when I rode, but I did not have to be. The combination of alcohol, late nights and insufficient sleep simply diminished my reaction time.

Of course, I never connected those dots. I heard Mack tell me he would be using other riders, without any lengthy explanation. Perhaps he did not have it in him to make mention of my drinking, although he'd certainly seen that lifeless, hungover look in my eyes enough mornings to be concerned.

I knew that two mistakes were two too many. Errors cannot be tolerated at the track because purse money—typically sixty percent for first place, twenty percent for second, ten percent for third, and five percent for fourth, with the rest distributed equally to the other starters—is counted on to offset the enormous daily cost of maintaining Thoroughbreds. At major circuits, owners typically spend several thousand dollars per month per horse for training and veterinary bills.

Still, I thought that Mack and Mr. Mellon and I had come too far together for me to get fired. I thought we had accomplished too much with horses such as Fit to Fight, who'd swept New York's Handicap Triple Crown by rolling through the Metropolitan, Suburban and Brooklyn handicaps. But no. Mack said that instead of depending on me, Mr. Mellon wanted to work from a list of jockeys. My name was not on the list.

I did not argue. I did not show any emotion even while I thought of the ramifications of the greatest setback of my career. I did ask that they keep me on Java Gold, a horse that was immensely talented but with a propensity for not changing leads.

When Thoroughbreds become fatigued, they typically switch their leg action so they can begin to use a different set of muscles. I had been diligently working with Java Gold in the morning to prompt him to make that change and he'd just been coming around. I knew he had big days ahead of him and wanted to be part of that—indeed, Java Gold would go on to win the 1987 Travers, one of the premier events for three-year-olds, at Saratoga Race Course. As much as I felt I deserved to be part of that celebration, that party went on without me.

Even as I grasped how completely the cord was being cut, I could not help but think of my strong ties to Mack, ties that no business decision could ever change. I had been enjoying a cup of coffee with him almost every morning since I started riding in New York. We connected the first time we met.

MACK: *I was training horses at Belmont Park one spring day when Jerry came in with his agent and introduced himself. I liked his countenance. He had a good face. He had a bright expression, a nice smile. He looked like he came from a good family.*

My father always told me, "Remember as you walk through life, you cannot get any whitewash on you if you do not rub against it." What he meant was keep your nose clean and associate with the nicest people you can. I knew right away that Jerry was someone I should rub against.

A couple of days later I told him to come in and have coffee with me. You call it camaraderie. I had a little kitchen near my office. We would sit around and shoot the bull. We'd have a cup of coffee and occasionally I'd get some sweet rolls. We'd tell a lot of lies, you know.

I could not think of anything I would rather do to start each day. Mack would talk, about horses and life, and I would take in every word. Just as Ray York had done years before, he drilled into me the importance of saving something for the end. He and Mr. Mellon emphasized stamina and endurance. Their horses were bred to go the classic distance of a mile and a quarter. They were trained to last. He did not want an impatient ride to undermine that.

"Jerry," he would tell me, "this is not the quarterhorse business. These horses have to run long."

All of those memories collided with the harsh reality of the present as I left the track that day. Only a few months before, we had purchased our first house, in Muttontown, New York. Five bedrooms, three acres, enough space to be comfortable, no matter how many children we decided to have. The mortgage, needless to say, matched the grandeur of the house.

Two thoughts dominated my drive home. What would I tell Suzee? How could I compensate for the lost income and keep the bank from foreclosing?

Predictably, Suzee handled the news better than I did. I cried and agonized about our future. She stayed strong and never lost her faith in me.

SUZEE: *Firing Jerry was one of the best things Mack could have done for him. He needed to learn that he could not get his way all the time. He needed to learn that owners and trainers could make do without him. There were other competent riders they could hire. I hoped this would humble him a bit.*

Although I was worried about where we were going to go or what would happen next, I always feel there is nothing Jerry cannot do. I kept reminding myself of that. I just felt everything would be okay, and I never wavered from that.

This was a wrong turn our marriage did not need. Even though Suzee never complained, she did not have to. I could see the stress in her face. As much as she reached out to me, as much as she tried to make me happy, I rarely reciprocated. I was too swept up in my routine—riding and drinking, drinking and riding—to take notice of her needs.

I was all about me, not we.

She lacked certain qualities that were very important to me. Promptness is one of them. I am on time to the minute, if not early. Not Suzee. She was an hour late for our wedding—her session with the photographer ran longer than expected, then she was caught in traffic on the often-snarled Long Island Expressway.

I kept my silence that day, but not after that.

Whenever she kept me waiting, which was often, I let her hear about it. I did not care what the circumstances were. I viewed her explanations, legitimate as they may have been, as excuses. The way I saw it, her lateness translated into disrespect for me. And I made damn sure that my wife did not disrespect me.

Even if Suzee did not often rebel, in the winter of 1988, her body began to. She developed extremely painful sores on her head and one that left her with a bloodshot eye. She was so uncomfortable she had to take to her bed.

When Suzee went to our doctor, he diagnosed her with shingles, but then as he prescribed treatment, he wanted to know the cause.

"Is something bothering you?" he asked.

Suzee shook her head no.

"Is there something you want to talk to me about?"

She could not bear to tell him about the tension that gripped our home life. I cringed when I saw her this way, even if it was only temporary. I knew I was the reason.

I had to do something, but that something never involved seeking the treatment I so desperately needed. I knew Suzee loved animals. Maybe a pet would help?

SUZEE: *He told me to pick out whatever I wanted. I settled on an adorable cocker spaniel named Barney. I doted over him as if he was our first child, and he rewarded my love tenfold. Barney helped me through so many awful times, starting with my nasty case of shingles.*

Those awful times were due to me. Almost every evening, I would turn into a monster before her eyes. I would return home tired from riding and hungry because the need to keep my weight down allowed me to take in so little food during the course of the day. It was essential that I have supper early so my body could burn off calories before I slept.

I must have explained this a thousand times. Still, dinner was late more nights than not. I let her hear about it every time, and the night would go downhill from there. My drinking would accelerate after supper. It was as if I transformed into her worst nightmare minute by minute. The blue eyes that had so deeply attracted her at first? They would become an angry red as my eyelids descended, leaving me a slit to see through as I stumbled around.

When we argued, I was liable to throw anything and everything I could get my hands on in Suzee's direction. I would always come just close enough to frighten and intimidate her, which was my intention. I never physically abused her. I did not have to. My verbal abuse stung her more sharply than any slap would have.

I knew every vulnerability and pounced on it.

She prided herself on her appearance. I insulted her appearance.

"You were thin when I met you. You worked out all the time," I would say. "Now look at you. You're getting fat. That's what happens when you don't work out."

Suzee did work out, of course, and she would push a little harder to please me. When she dropped a few pounds, I would complain she was too thin.

My wife was not good at handling money, spending more than she needed on clothes, shoes, handbags, you name it. She was the first to admit this shortcoming. More ammunition for me.

"When I married you, you had debts," I would shout at her. "I bailed you out."

Suzee would gently remind me of the well-paying opportunities she had given up to share in my career. It was as if she had never spoken. I treated a few credit-card obligations as if she were wanted by the law. It was all about control. The more I yelled, the more control I felt I had.

"Where would you be without me?" I would bellow. "You'd have nothing if it wasn't for me."

Suzee was constantly trying to put an end to trouble at the track that I started.

SUZEE: *Jerry is so hard on himself. He expects perfection from himself. He expects the people around him— the owner, the trainer, his agent—to be perfect. When they were not, it used to be a major problem.*

Riding horses is only one aspect of a jockey's job. Another is public relations. Even though we have agents, when a jockey takes the time to sell himself to trainers and owners, the rewards can be great.

Flattery is not my forte. Neither is diplomacy. I could be as direct as my father—and every bit as hurtful. If a horse disappointed me at Saratoga, I would not think twice about dismounting and saying, "This horse belongs at Finger Lakes," a track, farther north in upstate New York, that is home to the tired and sore.

If an owner had spent hundreds of thousands on a horse only to be beaten by a much cheaper counterpart, I never thought twice about saying, "This horse isn't worth a damn." And that is the cleaned-up version. Then I would storm off while Suzee tried to smooth over my lack of consideration.

Not that I appreciated her efforts. When we got home and alcohol began to take over, I would berate her. "Don't think you can change me overnight. Stay out of my business. You're getting involved in things you know nothing about."

Other times, Suzee would be deep in conversation with an owner or trainer who was a major client. I would nudge her. "We've got to go." If she did not immediately part company, I would shout, "We've got to go now!" and all but drag her off.

The winter of 1987 was hellish for both of us. Just as Suzee was recovering from shingles, I was involved in an accident at Gulfstream Park in a race I was not even supposed to ride. The jockey had taken off sick, and the trainer pleaded with me to pick up the mount.

My willingness to help quickly backfired. Qui Prince broke down, leaving me with three broken ribs and a punctured lung— not only could I not ride, I couldn't even fly. Suzee came from New York to retrieve me. The favor I did that trainer kept me sidelined for almost two months. Those were two long months for me. They were even longer for my wife. My behavior always worsened when I was idle.

THE LOSS OF MACK MILLER'S SUPERB OUTFIT, COMBINED with my injury, could have snowballed into something very damaging to my career. It happens all the time that a rider falls out of grace with one stable, then another, then another, until he has no live mounts whatsoever.

With a huge assist from John Veitch, I made sure that did not happen to me. I respected Mack's decision, but I was not going to go away quietly. I was not going to go away, period.

Veitch trained for Darby Dan, which meant he could walk up

and down his shedrow and peer in at nothing but quality Thoroughbreds. When Mack let me go, Veitch immediately saw it as an opportunity and moved in. We clicked at once, which helped me immensely. Many New York trainers then took the attitude that if I was good enough for John Veitch, I was good enough for them.

John saddled a couple of excellent grass fillies, Plenty of Grace and Graceful Darby, and they helped me build my reputation as an outstanding turf rider. They were extremely responsive fillies, willing to sit in the pocket, then squeeze through the narrowest of openings with a burst of acceleration. They never failed to make me look good at a time when that was imperative.

The only negative aspect about my success with John was that it sent me the wrong message. I convinced myself that my drinking had had nothing to do with losing Mack's business. I could continue to hit the bottle and function well enough.

Alcoholics are very good at believing what they want to believe. They see the world the way they want to see it because that is so much easier than putting themselves in the position of others.

I never stopped and thought about the qualities that allowed a jockey like Angel Cordero to dominate. I never said to myself, "I can do the same thing, and I am going to do it." I do remember once asking Eddie Maple, a very capable rider, about what it took to make a good living in New York. He answered, "I worked hard, stood in line and waited for my turn to come."

I figured my turn would come, no matter how I acted.

In early 1988, I made the decision to compete in Arkansas. It was a good move professionally because I rode for Bob Holthus, one of the state's leading trainers, and we did well together. It was also an opportunity to team with Proper Reality, a three-year-old that Bob was excited about.

I quickly caught his Derby Fever when we won the Southwest Stakes. Then came the Arkansas Derby, the first major test. Proper Reality went off as a prohibitive favorite and the other riders treated us that way. They positioned themselves to keep us boxed inside.

I had tested the track previously and monitored the races I did not ride to see how the Oaklawn Park surface was playing. The rail was deep and dead. No one wanted any part of it. This thought kept recurring as I sat mid-pack, pinned inside, with no chance to slip out. When we reached the far turn, Proper Reality knew it was time to go. I knew it was time to go. But I was trapped behind a wall of horses with no opening other than the dreaded rail.

So I went for it. There was no other option. I am not one to sit there and accept defeat or hope to pick up just a piece of the purse. I ride to win. And that is exactly what I did with Proper Reality. He drove along the rail and—deep and dead, or not—romped home.

I was ecstatic. I'd been eighteenth in the 1982 Kentucky Derby with New Discovery and a distant ninth with Conquistarose in 1987, but now I was going to the Kentucky Derby with a legitimate chance. After being on two starters who were not nearly good enough, every bone in my body told me Proper Reality and I could get the job done.

My chief rivals were Winning Colors and Forty Niner. Although fillies generally do not attempt to go against the boys in the Derby, Winning Colors was no ordinary filly. She possessed dangerous speed, even at a mile and a quarter, and I was sure her trainer, D. Wayne Lukas, would have her primed for the race of her life, and her jockey, Gary Stevens, would know just how to nurse along her speed. Forty Niner, saddled by crafty Woody Stephens and ridden by steady Pat Day, was another threat.

Proper Reality? The crowd that jammed the Churchill Downs stands and infield did not know how deadly dull that rail had been when he took that path to skip home in the Arkansas Derby. They essentially dismissed him at 27–1. I knew better.

Proper Reality was the twelfth horse to enter the starting gate, with Winning Colors just to our inside. Forty Niner was the farthest outside, in post 17. My mount was very manageable, not headstrong at all. I knew I could place him wherever I wanted. When the bell rang, he broke alertly and I chose to sit six or seven lengths off the pace that I knew would be set by Lukas's filly.

Derby victories almost always involve a clean trip around the first turn. To my delight, that is what we got. No bumps. No bruises. My hopes were soaring.

As we wheeled into the backside, I took a close look at Winning Colors. My heart sank. She was on the lead, just as I'd expected, but to my dismay, she was moving with the greatest of ease, with no pressure whatsoever. Meanwhile, I had thought Day would make his presence felt with Forty Niner, but Pat wanted no part of any speed duel. Typically for him, he elected to sit patiently and trust his colt's ability to get there at the end.

Everything told me that Winning Colors was a special filly that would not come back to us. If anyone was going to beat her, someone had to go after her. I would have to be that someone.

I eased my hold on Proper Reality and he began to close ground, advancing from tenth after the opening quarter of a mile to fifth after half a mile. We were second when we hit the mile mark and still pushing. Stevens was feeling the heat. I saw him prompt his mount, asking her for a bit more.

I thought I had the measure of Winning Colors. I thought Proper Reality would kick on by. But it was not to be. I'd had to make the move much earlier than I wanted to, and it took too much out of him. He began to slow, and Forty Niner just blew by. He would miss nailing Winning Colors by only a neck. Risen Star closed for third. We were fourth. We just did not have quite enough at the end.

Still, we'd been fourth at the Kentucky Derby! Next time? I knew there'd be a next time.

THE TIME IN ARKANSAS WAS GOOD FOR MY CAREER, BUT not my marriage. Suzee accompanied me to Arkansas and I made sure we had nice accommodations, but after that, my concern for her pretty much ended.

Since she did not know anyone there, she looked to me to entertain her. I was the wrong guy for that. I was there to ride. When I wasn't working, I wanted to play. In this case, that usually meant drinking alone.

Suzee had an awful lot of time to herself in Arkansas, time to think about everything she had given up for my sake, time to have serious doubts about whether it was all worth it.

SUZEE: The way I saw it, I gave up a glamorous job and a very promising career. I had gone from celebrity to virtual anonymity. It hurt.

It hit me hard that there was nothing I could do that would please Jerry. In his eyes, everything I did was wrong. I started questioning myself in every regard. Maybe my husband's drinking was *my fault. Maybe I was nagging, interfering. If I walked on eggshells for a while and stayed out of his way, maybe he would cut back.*

I wanted Suzee around, yet I did not want her around. I wanted her to be home when I returned at night. I liked knowing my wife was with me. Just not too close.

With so much time to think and so little to do in Arkansas, Suzee understood, more than ever before, the one-sided nature of our relationship. I was an occasional companion, not a husband. I was not living the vows I had mouthed on our wedding day. I did not understand how badly I was falling short. Worst of all, I did not care.

Suzee gave up all hope of trying to get through to me. Approximately ten days into our Arkansas stay, she called my agent, Bob Frieze. She was sobbing. "We need help," she told him. "Jerry's got a drinking problem."

Bob did not know how to respond. He was not a counselor. His job, after all, was to line up the best possible mounts for me each day, nothing more. Bob made sure Suzee was okay, that I was not threatening her in any way, but there really was not much more he could do, given the nature of our business relationship.

Suzee was in despair. I did not realize it, of course, but we were one big argument away from a breakup, and that is what happened.

SUZEE: *I can fight with the best of them, but it gets to a certain level and I just melt. Words can hurt so bad.*

I don't even remember what it was about, but it doesn't matter. When Suzee started packing her belongings and told me she was leaving, I could tell she was hoping I would say or do something that would keep her from leaving. I did not. In fact, I thought it was a good idea.

All of our arguing was taking its toll on me, too. The idea of consuming all the vodka I wanted and not having to hear about it was, frankly, appealing to me just then. Honey, if you want to leave, be my guest.

Suzee could not wait to put Arkansas behind her. She loaded up the car and set out for St. Petersburg, Florida, to stay with her brother, Jack. With every passing mile, her mind became more jumbled.

SUZEE: *Part of being a controlling personality is that you keep others on edge all the time. Jerry had me on edge as never before. I depended on him for everything. What was I going to do now?*

I started thinking of my shortcomings. Maybe if I corrected those, Jerry would stop drinking. Maybe if I was on time more often and took better care of the house, he would pay more attention to me and give me the approval I longed for as a former actress. Jerry wanted perfection. What could I do to be perfect so we could get our lives back together?

Suzee's parents met her halfway between Arkansas and St. Petersburg. She spent three weeks at her brother Jack's house, contacting local television stations about job possibilities and trying to get herself back together emotionally.

SUZEE: *I remember sitting on my brother's dock and watching the sun set. I reviewed every aspect of my life. Who I was, where I came from, what I wanted more than anything else. I was filled with*

insecurity. Jerry's incessant criticism had taken a toll on my confi-
dence. I had lost touch with important contacts. I had no place to live.

As the sun began to dip out of sight, I prayed for answers, as I had
so many times before. As I walked the dock back to the house, I knew
I would return to Jerry. I did not want a bitter divorce, even if it
meant I would be well provided for. I would reunite with my hus-
band for the reason I think so many abused wives go back—they see
no other option.

Our weeks apart allowed me to think about who I was and
what I was going to do about it. I was an alcoholic. No one
needed to tell me that. I knew it just as I was sure that I needed to
quit. I just did not know how.

If I entered a rehabilitation program, I thought, everyone
would learn of a problem I had worked hard to conceal. As my
career progressed, I had been very careful not to drink with
other jockeys and trainers. I always thought other people were
out to hold me down, anyway. I did not want them to have anything they could use against me.

I was also gripped by the fear that I would lose everything I had
worked so hard for. I thought it would be ruinous if my very private problem became public.

If you had invested several hundred thousand dollars on a
regally bred horse, would you entrust him in a million-dollar
stakes race to someone who might be hopelessly hungover?

No, my secret had to remain just that.

I persuaded Suzee that things would be better and we recon-
ciled. By the Fourth of July, however, nothing had changed.

My mistreatment of Suzee was very obvious now. No longer

was it limited to times when we were alone. I do not even remember the issue, but I lit into her during a holiday picnic attended by another jockey, Randy Romero, and his wife, Cricket.

Cricket is a very straightforward woman. She will not hold back if she does not like what she is seeing. And she was repulsed by my verbal abuse.

"Does he treat you this way all the time?" Cricket asked Suzee.

My wife's embarrassment would soon boil over into anger. I had told her I was no longer consuming alcohol, and she chose to believe me. But, tired and thirsty as she cleaned up at the end of the picnic, she sipped from my glass, assuming it was a clear soft drink, and—

Straight vodka.

Suzee gagged, disgusted as much by my deception as by the unexpected alcohol. There could be no more hiding, no more running from the truth. When she confronted me, tears welled in my eyes as I acknowledged to her, for the first time, what I already had admitted to myself.

"I have a problem," I told her.

I decided to see a priest with whom we were friendly, Father Costa, at St. Paul's Church in Brookville, Long Island.

Father Costa was a good listener as I detailed years of excess.

"I would like to be able to help you," he said, "but I can't."

Instead he informed me that Alcoholics Anonymous held regular meetings at the church and recommended that I contact Tom, a member of that organization. Tom related to me how AA had helped him, gave me the schedule of meetings and urged me to attend. I went the next night.

The session, held in St. Paul's basement, was already under way when I arrived. I remember going to the door and hearing people laughing and carrying on. I was saddened. I thought to myself, *I don't know if I'm ready to quit drinking, but I sure want to be as happy as those people.*

I went inside, sat in the back and listened. I wanted to go unnoticed, and succeeded in that. I did not wish to participate. No one put any pressure on me to join the conversation. I listened as various members described how alcoholism had ruined their lives . . . and decided I had heard enough. This wasn't for me.

I'd arrived late, and I left early.

After that, twice a week, I told Suzee I was going to St. Paul's for an AA meeting, knowing that it would bring a measure of tranquillity to our relationship. And in fact, I always got as far as the door. But I never entered. If I could not stop drinking, I decided, I would simply hide it better.

Despite all the assurances I was giving Suzee, I was still thirsty. I was not ready to put it down yet.

As our marriage lurched along, we both felt the need for support. As Christmas approached, we joined my sister Kathy for skiing in Colorado. If there was ever a time to be sober, I knew this was the time. But I could not help myself. My alcoholism all but grabbed me by the arm and pulled me out of the ski lodge into the cold of night. I mumbled an excuse that was so familiar to Suzee by now.

"We need some things in the house. I'll run a few errands."

I returned an hour later, having taken care of one need, my desire for alcohol. There was no chance to hide what I had done. I all but fell through the door to announce my arrival. I reeked of alcohol.

Suzee had been telling Kathy about my problem. Now, my sister saw for herself the extent of it. The staggering evidence was in front of her.

"Look at your brother! Just look at him!" Suzee exclaimed to Kathy.

There was no defense for my deception. I certainly had not enjoyed myself during that one-hour binge. I had simply yielded to what my body and mind demanded.

Drinking was never a source of pleasure anymore. It had become a burden with what I had to go through to buy it and drink it, all the while attempting to conceal what I was doing from my wife, family members and co-workers.

Most people would say if it is not fun, just don't do it. Those people have no clue what addiction means. It is not nearly that easy.

Once I had recovered from my latest escapade, Suzee pushed me to act. "Why don't we stop this right here," she said, "and get you into a treatment center? You've already taken the time off. You've got three weeks to do this."

It all made sense. I could not dispute her on any point.

But no.

Suzee continued to press her case when we went on to spend Christmas with other members of my family at Kathy's house in Wyoming. Either they truly did not know I had a problem or they were in denial. After hearing my wife's plea that they join her in pushing me to get help, they treated her as if she was the one who was sick.

That only emboldened me as Suzee and I completed our vacation in the Cayman Islands. She continued to insist that I enter rehab. I continued to drink.

"I really don't need to do this," I insisted. "You know how strong I am. I will take care of it."

I ended the discussion there because that is the way I was. Once I reached a decision, there was no chance to persuade me otherwise. There was no talking to me, period.

With Christmas ruined, it was on to New Year's Eve. It should come as no surprise that we spent that time apart. Suzee visited her parents in Tampa. I was alone in a house we had rented in South Florida while I rode the winter meet at Gulfstream Park.

That was when she called me on New Year's Day, and I insisted, through slurred speech, that I absolutely had not been drinking. That was when she came to the house and found me passed out on the couch, and had so much difficulty rousing me from my drunken slumber that she thought I was dead.

When I was finally coherent, she confronted me with the evidence of the marked gin bottle. And that was when I finally admitted, after years of futility, that alcoholism was one thing Jerry Bailey could not handle.

As I looked at Suzee's sweet, tear-stained face, I had no doubt I was going to lose my wife if I did not seek treatment.

"You are right. I have been drinking," I said. "I need help."

And help was on the way.

Six

THE ENEMY WITHIN

*M*y time had come.

I had been sitting in a circle and listening as others introduced themselves and told how years of excess had harmed their health, cost them family and friends, and all but destroyed their lives.

The speaker next to me was finished. It was time to tell anyone within earshot a secret I had carefully hidden for so long.

"Hi, my name is Jerry," I began, "and I'm an alcoholic."

The words came easily. By now, the fact that I was Jerry Bailey, a prominent jockey, did not give me reason to pause. I was nothing more or less than any other person who was sick and needed help.

There was comfort in the circle. While I needed to be willing to fight the enemy within for my recovery, I was not wading into battle alone.

I soon learned to take solace in the Serenity Prayer.

"God grant us the serenity to accept/the things we cannot change,/ The courage to change the things we can,/And the wisdom to know the difference."

The Serenity Prayer is typically followed by the preamble, which describes Alcoholics Anonymous as "a fellowship of men and women who share their experiences, strength and hope with each other that they may solve their common problem and help others to recover from alcoholism.

"The only requirement for membership is a desire to stop drinking. There are no dues or fees for Alcoholics Anonymous membership; we are self-supporting through our own contributions. Alcoholics Anonymous is not allied with any sect, denomination, politics, organization or institution, does not wish to engage in any controversy, neither endorses nor opposes any causes. Our primary purpose is to stay sober and help other alcoholics to achieve sobriety."

For someone like me, who yearns for control, I was overwhelmed by my powerlessness against alcoholism, but drew strength from the company of others. This is no wound that heals. There is no medicine that will lead to a cure, because it is impossible to change a person's body chemistry.

Alcoholism is forever.

In one sense, the key to recovery is so simple. According to the American Medical Association, "Treatment primarily involves not taking a drink." But that is precisely why some alcoholics allow their disease to progress until they die of cirrhosis of the liver or perhaps kill themselves and innocent people in fiery car accidents.

It can be unbelievably difficult not to take that one drink. Day-by-day only begins to describe the battle; for many, the fight is hour-by-hour. If there is a slip, if an alcoholic takes one drink, it inevitably leads to many.

That is why the theme "If you don't take that first drink, you can't get drunk" is heard repeatedly at AA meetings.

When I joined Terry's program, it was so hard for me to conceive of the fact that I would have to go the rest of my life consuming nothing harder than a soft drink. So much of each day had been built around alcohol. Where would I buy it? Where would I consume it? How would I hide it from others at the racetrack? How would I keep it from Suzee?

The more I studied the subject, the clearer it became that there is no margin for error. Through the years, I have come to fully understand the wisdom of a statement the American Medical Association issued in 1964:

"Alcohol, aside from its addictive qualities, also has a psychological effect that modifies thinking and reasoning. One drink can change the thinking of an alcoholic so that he feels he can tolerate another, and then another, and another. . . .

"The alcoholic can learn to completely control his disease, but the affliction cannot be cured so that he can return to alcohol without adverse consequences."

For my wife, too, life was changing permanently. She had suspected my alcoholism for years, always hoping somehow that it was not true despite evidence that was before her almost nightly. I had been in denial for an equal amount of time. Now, I was acknowledging my problem. That meant she had to face it, too.

As I mentioned in the first chapter, when we went to dinner with Terry Grant to learn more about his program, he emphasized to me and Suzee that alcoholism was not my disease. It was our disease. If I was to recover, she needed to be as much a part of the process as I was.

As much as Suzee loved me, as much as she was devoted to me, this was all very difficult for her to hear and absorb. She decided to spend time with old friends in California, and I was fine with that. I was finally in a good place mentally. She needed to join me there.

SUZEE: *I felt I needed some time to find myself. I needed to ask myself, "Why did you stay in this so long? Where is this marriage going?"*

I know it may look like I took my toys and ran, but going to California was probably the best thing I could have done. I thought about our tumultuous past and what would be necessary for us to put our marriage and our lives back together. Both of us would need formal treatment. It would take time to get well. The only answer was to move forward together.

I flew back to Florida and began attending Al-Anon meetings. The first few times I introduced myself, the words came haltingly.

"Hi, I'm Suzee," I would begin before drawing a deep breath. "And I'm married to an alcoholic."

Al-Anon sessions were initially very uncomfortable for me. I had been taught not to hang out your dirty laundry. Do not show the world your weaknesses. Do not reveal your troubles to those who do not know you well. Now, there I was, hanging my dirty laundry everywhere.

It was embarrassing to relate to strangers the awful insults my husband used to hurl at me. The retelling made me hurt all over again. But I also saw that what I was learning about the disease was gradually replacing despair with hope in our home.

I had been building emotional walls from the time I noticed signs that Jerry might have a problem. Now I was opening doors. With the help of a wonderful sponsor, Phyllis, it was reinforced that I did not cause my husband's problem. I could not cure it. He would have to do that himself. For the sake of both of us, it was time that I focused on me.

Many alcoholics, as hard as they fight to stay sober, suffer relapses. What would I do if that happened? How would I cope with the everyday stresses that alcoholism brings?

When it came time for Jerry to make amends, for me that meant reliving years of misery. As he reviewed with me the different places he would buy liquor, where he would go to drink it and the lies he would tell to cover it all, I could not believe the degree to which I had been duped.

He admitted that some of his satisfaction came from deceiving me so completely. And I began to wonder, "If he lied to me about drinking, what else had he lied to me about?" I had to find a way to trust him, and it wasn't easy.

He assured me he had always remained faithful and I had no proof to the contrary. Sadly, there had been many nights when I sought intimacy—only to see that he was sleeping it off.

At the same time, as I saw Jerry making confessions to family members and friends, some of whom were as much in denial as I had been, I saw how good and strong he could be. I was reminded all over again of why I married him and hung in there for so long. He had dedicated himself fully to his recovery. As difficult as it was, I had to do the same.

I enjoyed almost instant results from Terry's program. Physically and emotionally, I felt better. My relationship with my wife was better. It also helped when I called different members of my family to make amends. In the case of my sister Becky, some of my behavior had been so childish, we could not help but laugh in recalling it.

BECKY: *We were playing Monopoly at my house in El Paso during a Christmas get-together late in the 1970s. We were all drinking vodka and orange juice. You would say we had indulged in our share of holiday cheer and then some.*

Jerry was not winning and, of course, he loves to win. He gradually started running out of Monopoly money until finally he was broke. He refused to leave the game gracefully. He whipped out his credit card, threw it on the board and shouted, "I'm going to keep playing."

When he realized we would not allow him to continue, no matter how big his credit line was compared to ours, he flipped over the game, bringing our holiday celebration to an unhappy end.

With most of my family members, the greatest harm done to them was through neglect. I had virtually disowned them since my mother's death. If they called, I always acted as if I had something more important to do than talk to them. If I called, well, that hardly ever happened.

When it came to my best friend, Bryan Fann, there was a long list of offenses that I reviewed and for which I asked forgiveness.

BRYAN: *He could get ignorant when he drank. He would get rude. I could see it coming.*

One night he got mad at me and threw a phone. I just ducked. The phone hit the wall and broke. I kept right on talking as though nothing had happened.

I know there were a lot of times he regretted things as soon as he did them. The difference is now he was apologizing for them. Then, he wouldn't have.

One time at a diner he said, "How did you put up with me and the things I did?" I said, "Because I love you, man." You don't throw a good friend away because he said or did something you didn't like. He was a good person and is a good person.

There is a saying that if you add alcohol, you have an instant idiot. Jerry shows how much you can change when you eliminate one thing.

Terry's program was designed to last for six weeks. I stayed for three months. It meant that much to me to hear other alcoholics tell their stories and know I was not alone. The meetings were never a burden. I enjoyed them. I can remember going through certain days and thinking, *I need a meeting.* They were something for me to hold on to, and I clung to them as if they were a life raft in a stormy sea.

I had made up my mind that I would not disclose to the media my alcoholism and my decision to enter an outpatient rehabilitation program. At the same time, if information leaked and I was presented with it, I would not shrink from the truth. I would confront it.

As it was, the other member of the racing community in the group respected my privacy. A number of years later, I finally told my story to Bill Nack, an award-winning writer from *Sports*

Illustrated, because I saw it as an opportunity to help others and was so sure he would handle it properly. He did not disappoint me.

Treating alcoholism involves so much more than attending meetings. I began to see how much alcohol pervades our daily lives. Liquor advertising, on billboards, on glossy magazine pages, now leaped out at me.

I had to brace myself whenever I flew to a major race, knowing that as soon as I settled into a first-class seat a stewardess would approach to ask, "Would you like anything to drink, today?" Would the words "No, thanks" always be at the tip of my tongue?

Alcoholism means changing so many aspects of your life, down to where you go and who you go with. Because I feared I would slip, I initially insisted that Suzee and I not go to restaurants. It used to be that I did not go anywhere for dinner unless that establishment served liquor.

We stayed away from social events for two years, which was particularly difficult for my wife because she is naturally gregarious. When I needed to travel for business, she accompanied me. It was the only way I could feel sure that I would stay in control.

Suzee suggested we both attend counseling in addition to our AA and Al-Anon meetings. I agreed. I had to learn to deal with everyday problems without having alcohol as a crutch and would need help with that. Life does not change when you quit drinking. The way you react to it does.

They say the moment you start drinking you stop growing emotionally. That put me at age seventeen or so. Believe me, I could be that immature, that rebellious.

Therapy sessions with Dr. John Klotche in New York helped both of us immensely. A few of our ongoing issues had rather simple solutions, such as our monthly spending. The answer, which had not been obvious to either of us before, was to establish a budget we could both live with.

We also came to see that we did not have to fight every battle until the bitter end. Some nights, it was okay to go to bed angry. Time can ease certain strains, if you just allow that to happen.

Suzee tended to bottle up her emotions. That was not healthy for our marriage. If she had something to say, it was up to her to say it.

She used to tiptoe around me on days when I rode major races, fearing that a dispute might affect my concentration and cause either a defeat or a devastating accident. All that had done was to encourage me to be even more controlling. She was helping to create the monster.

I was taught to acknowledge my shortcomings and address them. In one exercise, we were asked to list our character flaws. *Short-tempered. Lack compassion. Lack patience.* Those topped my list.

In time, I understood it was not always what I said that upset others. It was how I said it. Honesty is valued. So is straightforwardness. But not when comments insult or hurt others. Emotional wounds are so much worse than physical wounds. If you hit someone and hurt that person, eventually a scab will form and drop off. When the damage is emotional, there is no telling when it is gone or if it ever disappears.

John taught me to value the phrase "good enough." I always wanted everything to be perfect, to go exactly as planned. How often does that happen? I had spent so much of my energy striving for perfection, demanding it from others and being frustrated and angry when we both fell short. While I will always pursue excellence in anything I do, I had to learn to value "good enough."

I was not a changed man overnight. I still have much work to do. I continue to strive to correct my flaws and imperfections, knowing that is a lifelong task for all of us. At least I was finally working at it, and sobriety was making all the difference.

SUZEE: *I've always believed that God does not give you more than you can handle. At last, we were handling our problems and it was as if we were newlyweds all over again. We embraced our new beginning as often as we embraced each other.*

We still argued but the intensity of the arguments began to diminish. Jerry's attitude used to be "Be reasonable, do it my way." Now, we compromised. He used to treat me as if he owned me because he paid my bills. Now, he knew my self-esteem required me to be more than Jerry Bailey's wife. I was a proud woman with my own abilities, my own identity.

As much as rehabilitation helped my marriage, the effect on my riding was equally dramatic. My tendency toward arrogance had been replaced by true confidence. It is not my place to name names, but there are many riders who drink during their free time, and it is not uncommon to see them drink too much. I was convinced sobriety was giving me a tremendous edge.

That showed itself in so many ways. The jockeys participate in a softball game in upstate New York every summer to benefit cancer research. I used to play the outfield and do more harm than good. If I charged in, the ball soared over my head. If I retreated a couple of steps, it fell in front of me. In the summer of 1989, however, I ran down every line drive, every looper.

Cordero noticed the difference.

"You taking lessons or something?" he asked playfully.

"Angel," I answered, "I'm seeing one ball instead of two."

That was the truth. My sudden aptitude as an outfielder reflected the dramatic change in my life. My preparation, always a strength, was even better. I looked at past performances and it was as if the race was unfolding before my eyes. I was able to see where every horse was likely to be placed at different stages. To my delight, this played out accurately time and time again.

My reaction time was awesome. My reflexes were sharper. Everything seemed to be moving five miles per hour, not ninety-five.

Riding was no longer just a job. It was becoming a great deal of fun. In the spring of 1989, I had a blast with Proper Reality in the $589,000 Metropolitan Handicap at New York's Belmont Park.

We were given a shot, but most of the win money went to a potent Ogden Phipps entry of front-running Seeking the Gold, with Pat Day, and Dancing Spree, who would close for Angel Cordero, Jr.

I bided my time behind Seeking the Gold. Angel sat chilly as well. By the time we reached the top of the lane, however, Dancing Spree had circled the field to draw nearly even with his stablemate, while I remained in excellent striking position.

I can only imagine Mr. Phipps's consternation as Day and Cordero, who did not like each other, used his horses to fight for all they were worth. I delighted in the unexpected duel, knowing what it could mean for Proper Reality. We pounced in the final furlong, rallying from one and a half lengths back.

The reputations of rough-and-tumble Cordero and the unflappable Day already were made. They were bound for the history books. This furious three-horse fight to the wire was my chance to show the world that Jerry Bailey could ride a little bit, too.

Pat had left something in the tank with Seeking the Gold. Angel was laying all over Dancing Spree. I was giving Proper Reality my all and he was reciprocating. Stride for stride, the three of us stayed together. I implored Proper Reality for more. Still no separation. I pushed Proper Reality's head forward as the three of us hit the wire and . . . too close to call.

Jockeys usually do not need photographic evidence to know the outcome. I was pretty sure I had gotten there first. A few minutes later, the eagerly awaited photo turned "pretty sure" into the biggest smile you would ever want to see.

We had crossed the line a whisker ahead of Seeking the Gold, who had been softened by a most unexpected source. Dancing Spree was another nose behind.

No one had to tell me how this result would affect the way owners and trainers viewed me. It was no mean feat to outride Cordero and Day to the wire, and yet the will and courage of Proper Reality had helped me accomplish that. I cannot say he was the best horse in the country in 1989. I am sure he fought harder than anyone else.

Then in 1990, my handiwork with a good three-year-old, Home at Last, brought my first victory in a million-dollar race. I was so committed to the colt that I elected to ride him in the Illinois Derby, which at the time was run the same day as the Kentucky Derby, rather than pursue a mount in the Run for the Roses.

Home at Last, trained by Carl Nafzger, was not nominated to the Kentucky Derby. At that stage, my attitude toward the opening leg of the Triple Crown was that I would go there to contend or win—or not go there at all. I just saw it as a good business decision. I've always understood that success in my chosen field depends on listening to your mind rather than your heart.

There was only one problem with my sound reasoning: It rained the night before the Illinois Derby. Nafzger and I spoke that evening and he immediately wanted to scratch. I pleaded with him to hold off on his decision because the horse could be pulled up until forty-five minutes before post time. There was no talking him out of it.

So I spent the first Saturday in May uncomfortable in my living room as I watched another Nafzger horse, Unbridled, ridden by Craig Perret, win the Kentucky Derby. The real kick in the pants, however, came when I checked on the Illinois Derby. The surface had dried during the day. By the time that race was run, the track condition was officially listed as fast. Home at Last had missed a good opportunity for no reason—and I had lost a potentially large payday.

It was not the only time Nafzger's actions made my blood boil. Later in the year, I stayed on Home at Last when he ran as an entry with Unbridled in the Super Derby in Louisiana. As we prepared for the race, it was clear that Carl had room in his mind for only one horse, and that was Unbridled.

My instructions were to prompt the pace, then do the best I could. In other words, to do everything you can to set up the big prize for Unbridled. And that was the last I saw or heard from the trainer. I helped the groom saddle the horse before the groom gave me a leg up. By the time we reached the track, I was fired up. I felt slighted. I thought more of myself and Home at Last than to be an afterthought. I would show them.

I rode Home at Last with more confidence than Carl ever

showed in him. We stayed close to the pace and he packed a punch when I asked him. Although Unbridled placed second, Nafzger was less than overjoyed with his one-two finish.

"The wrong horse won," I overheard him say.

However, nothing could spoil that moment for me. It was my first victory in a million-dollar race. I received $60,000, or ten percent of $600,000, the winner's share of the purse. The significance was not lost on me.

Suzee and I were finally starting to feel less strain financially. Just a couple of years earlier, we had been going from paycheck to paycheck to make sure we could make a hefty mortgage payment. And I had not forgotten, nor will I ever forget, that I risked life and limb to exercise horses for two dollars a head when I started.

So many athletes lose perspective as their financial power increases. They allow friends to become dependents. They buy cars and mansions as if they are picking up socks and underwear. They cannot own enough toys.

The large numbers attached to each paycheck can be numbing. I never allowed that to happen. I felt fortunate that in a couple of minutes I could earn what it takes many people a year to bring home from the job. At the same time, I never lost sight of the enormous risk I took every time I sat in the starting gate.

As I thought of what Home at Last had done in allowing me to celebrate my first million-dollar victory, it would have been more fitting if he had been named Peace at Last. I did not feel any urge to celebrate with alcohol.

My regular attendance at AA meetings, which followed three months in rehabilitation, was making a difference. When laughter filled those meetings, I was no longer standing outside and peering in, wishing I could be happy the way they were.

I was enjoying the moment, too.

Only God can know if rehabilitation spared me paralysis or death on the racetrack. I can only be grateful that I changed my lifestyle when I did.

Seven

COPING WITH INFERTILITY: OUR ANSWERED PRAYER

*A*lcohol was not my only personal battle at that time.
When asked during my outpatient program to list my greatest fear, it had nothing to do with perils that are part of a jockey's everyday existence.

Half-ton Thoroughbreds? The most mean-spirited of them could not intimidate me.

Competing at high speeds? Loved it.

Failure? Never contemplated it.

There was one fear that gripped me and I immediately wrote it down: "I fear that I will never be able to father a child."

That was all, but it was worse than anything else I could imagine. Having a child was that important to Suzee and me. We had discussed our desire to start a family almost as soon as we both realized we were in love, which was early in courtship. She wanted four children. I thought three was a better number.

When we purchased that first house, in Muttontown, with its five bedrooms and three acres, we'd expected that most of those rooms would soon be full. We delighted in our spacious backyard, knowing it would give our children ample room to romp and play.

We'd hoped Suzee would conceive as soon as we were married and so hadn't practiced any form of birth control. When nothing happened in the first couple of years, though, we were not overly concerned. We were both beginning to recognize the hold that alcoholism had on me. The issue was foremost on both of our minds. Suzee had moments when she wondered if it was in her interest to have a child with me, knowing that represented more of a commitment to our faltering relationship. Frankly, there were plenty of nights when I was too drunk for us even to try.

By 1988, however, it was very obvious that infertility was a problem. We both consulted our personal physicians and our ride on an emotional roller coaster began.

My job, with the travel it required from one meet to another and then to major races in between, only increased the difficulty of finding an answer. A large number of doctors became involved. Each, it seemed, formed a different opinion. As soon as we started to make progress with one physician, it was time to move on to another track and another city.

While we were open to adoption and explored that option, we had reservations about proceeding. We did not want to fall in love with a little girl or boy only to have one of the natural parents decide he wanted his offspring back.

Beyond that, we still thought we could have a child of our own because that is what doctors were leading us to believe. Still, they struggled to explain why we had repeatedly failed.

We were prepared to go to any lengths in our urgent search for answers. There were mornings when I worked horses at Belmont Park, then withdrew to the relative privacy of my car in a remote parking lot to produce a sperm sample that I would drive to Manhattan for testing. Of course, I might have had a hard time convincing a security officer of my purpose if I had ever been spotted.

Another time, Suzee and I were getting ready to board a flight in Miami when we realized she was due for an injection. It was vital to keep to the schedule if her fertility was to rise to an optimal level. We found a remote part of the terminal and retreated to a janitor's closet, where I injected her upper hip.

Giving those shots was as painful as being on the receiving end. The schedule of injections was so frequent that her hip area turned various shades of purple. I had to search for a spot that was not bruised or settle for one depth of purple that was lighter than another. Suzee never complained and neither did I. We would do almost anything to get pregnant. The longer it went without happening, the deeper our yearning became.

Doctors eventually concluded that we were dealing with two sets of problems. Suzee's uterus was tilted, and my sperm was lackadaisical and did not always reach the egg as quickly as desired. In an effort to increase the number of eggs available for fertilization and to add to the quantity of sperm attempting to reach those eggs, we each tried fertility drugs.

Still, nothing.

Suzee, born on December 2, 1958, was in her thirties now and we both heard the loud ticking of her biological clock. While we turned to science, we also relied on our faith. A friend, Tommy Fischetti, visited Rome and arranged for a novena, or a set of prayers, to be said on our behalf. He brought back a blessed set of rosary beads that I kept with me often.

Beginning in 1991, Suzee endured a painful procedure called artificial insemination. A long tube was used to place my sperm as close as possible to her ovaries. The process was repeated several times.

Still, nothing.

We were beginning to run out of avenues to explore.

That was when Dr. Mina Selub in Miami told us about a rare procedure known as GIFT, gamete intrafallopian transfer. Fertility drugs were again used to spur the development of more eggs. Since Suzee's fallopian tubes were healthy, the eggs and sperm were combined and immediately placed there so that fertilization could occur normally.

There was only one hitch. If the process is successful, doctors generally perform selective abortion to control the number of babies a patient will have. In Suzee's case, four eggs were used to increase the chances of pregnancy. We were not willing to allow any of them to be destroyed and made that clear at the outset.

SUZEE: *We were trying to stir life in my womb and now a doctor was talking about taking one or more lives? Jerry and I both oppose abortion. Common sense tells us a life is created at the moment of conception. We abhor the taking of any life, beginning with embryos.*

We felt as though we were asking God for a miracle. As much as we knew Dr. Selub was doing everything she could to enhance our chances, we were not about to try to control that miracle. We would have been haunted for the rest of our lives if we had authorized the elimination of one or more of our potential children.

As it was, we wished we could conceive our child without the intervention of modern medicine, without drugs and petri dishes and incubators. At the same time, we felt a divine spirit was merely working through doctors who were trying so hard to help us.

GIFT did not come with any guarantees. It was another attempt to improve our odds, just as everything else had been. The four eggs were implanted. The waiting began.

Finally, it was time for Suzee to submit to a blood test. We were guardedly optimistic, knowing our hopes had been dashed before. We prayed and braced ourselves. We were prepared if the news should be disappointing again.

Suzee was pregnant! It was as if the heavens had opened. The level of excitement we experienced surpassed any race result. This was life itself, the life of the child we had tried to conceive for seven years and had started to think we would never have.

Then joy gave way to fear and anxiety. What if there was a miscarriage? What if we wanted this gift more than God wanted us to have it? My wife was almost afraid to move. I touched her as if she were fine china.

SUZEE: *My pregnancy brought out in Jerry all the good qualities I had always believed were there but were overpowered by alcoholism. As I gained weight with each passing month and worried that I was no longer appealing, he assured me I was more beautiful than ever in his eyes.*

Always a planner, he thought of everything that would make our child happy and safe. He padded corners of the walls. He put clips on all of the bedroom drawers, so a toddler could not open them. He placed a ladder in the nursery to provide a quick escape in case of fire.

It was a wonderful new chapter in our lives. I never felt so loved, by both Jerry and our friends. Tina Mott, whose husband, Bill, is a prominent trainer, was constantly there for me. She shared my blood type and donated blood in case it was needed. She hosted a baby shower that so shocked me I thought I would have our son on the spot. Tina was there for me in every way. I will never forget her for that.

We held our breath with each checkup. On the first visit after the pregnancy was confirmed, it was thought there might be two heartbeats. On the next visit, there was only one heartbeat, but it was strong and growing stronger all the time. I accompanied Suzee for her first sonogram and vividly remember our jubilation.

The spot on the screen, that was our child!

It was too soon to tell whether she was carrying a girl or a boy. That would come with the next sonogram. Although our most fervent desire was to have a healthy newborn, I must admit I wished for a boy. I wanted someone who would share my love of sports, who would watch a football game with me and care as deeply about the outcome as I did. When we learned we would have a son, that was the cherry on top.

I was so proud of Suzee. She was careful about what she ate and took great care of herself. She read everything she could get her hands on concerning infant care and what it would take to raise our son. She was as prepared as a first-time mother could possibly be.

The pregnancy followed a normal course until we went past

our November 17 due date. After a week, it was decided to perform a Caesarean section. Suzee was given the option of having it done before or immediately after Thanksgiving.

We enjoyed a Thanksgiving meal that was charged with meaning. I toasted the holiday with nothing stronger than bottled water. Our marriage had been saved. Our seven-year wait to start a family was about to end.

The next day, Suzee entered the hospital to have labor induced. Twenty-seven long hours later, and after a brief concern because monitors showed the baby's heart was in a bit of distress, Justin Daniel Bailey was born, on November 28, 1992.

"Wow, he's a big boy!" the doctor exclaimed as he cradled nine-pound, nine-ounce Justin.

I could not believe my eyes. He looked messy but great. A career's worth of highlights could not surpass the exhilaration of that moment. My joy was matched only by an enormous sense of relief because, after countless failed attempts, we had so feared that something might go wrong.

"Let me see him!" Suzee pleaded. "Will somebody please let me see my baby?"

SUZEE: *The first thing I could make out were his little eyes. They were steely, grayish black. He looked right through us, like he knew us before we knew him. After all of our years of doubt and heartache, it was as if this moment was meant to happen all along.*

I'll never forget how proud Jerry was the next day. He was standing next to a tall, stocky man who gazed lovingly into a crib that contained a tiny newborn. Jerry, all five feet, five inches, 112 pounds of him, pointed to the biggest baby on the ward.

"That's mine!" he said, as his shirt buttons all but popped loose.

I don't know if I can put into words what it meant to bring Justin home. Our five-bedroom house had felt so empty. Motherhood was something I had started to think I would never experience. Holding our child was like holding a piece of heaven.

Jerry gently bathed him for the first time. The new member of our family looked so fragile, I was almost afraid to touch him. He was baptized the day after Christmas.

Jerry was due to ride the winter meet at Gulfstream Park in Florida, so our son experienced his first plane ride a month after he was born. He was already a racetracker

When Justin was a year old, we began to explore the possibility of having a second child with the aid of the GIFT procedure. A mammogram, however, revealed a cyst in Suzee's right breast. It turned out to be benign, but it gave both of us reason to pause.

We were concerned about possible long-term ramifications if my wife took more fertility drugs. We had prayed for a child to carry on our name. We had received a child. We regarded that alarming mammogram as a sign from God that we should devote all of our energies to Justin and be wholly satisfied with all that he has meant to us.

When our son was five or six, he used to ask why he did not have any brothers or sisters. We did everything we could to make sure he was never lonely. We arranged playdates with his friends and made sure there were always plenty of other children around him. In time, he knew how much he was loved and became content with life as an only child.

When Justin was four or five years old, he started to notice that I would leave the house at least several nights a week.

"Where are you going?"

"To a meeting," I would tell him.

"What for?"

"To help me not drink," I would answer.

"What else do you go there for?"

"To help me feel good."

Even little Justin saw how much AA was helping me, even if he knew nothing about the organization or the gravity of my problem. Sometimes, when I was having a bad day or was short-tempered, he would tell me, "Dad, maybe you need to go to a meeting."

I tried to explain to Justin about alcoholism when he was still at a young age. I know he will have to live his own life and make his own choices. I have tried to make it abundantly clear to him that lives are irreparably harmed by bad decisions. If you get in a car and the driver has been drinking or using drugs, awful things can happen to you, your passengers and innocent bystanders.

JUSTIN: *I've never seen my dad drunk. When I go to baseball tournaments with my travel team, I see others drink. I'm always happy when he doesn't join them.*

When I was younger, my father was angrier. Now, he doesn't get mad so easily. He doesn't get mad for the wrong reasons. I'm proud of him for being able to change.

As Justin grew older, I found myself increasingly torn between my family's needs and the extensive travel my career required. Retirement became more and more appealing. While Suzee did everything she could to play the role of mom and dad, taking him here and there, encouraging him when that was needed, chastising him when he deserved it, the time away became hard for me.

Although cell phones are great, they can only do so much. Hearing his excited voice tell me about one of his baseball or soccer games was not the same as seeing what he had done. Telling him long-distance how proud I was fell way short of looking into his eyes and letting him know that.

Wishing him good night and reassuring him that I would be home soon was not the same as embracing him before I turned off his light.

No matter how many winners I had ridden that day, there were so many nights in so many hotel rooms when I would have given anything to hug my son and fall asleep next to my wife.

Eight

SOARING TO
UNIMAGINED HEIGHTS

*T*he winners, however, did keep on coming.

When baseball sluggers refer to being "in the zone," it means they see the ball clearly from the instant it leaves the pitcher's hand. They understand its rotation, and they watch it come close, larger and larger, as if in slow motion, until they swing the bat and make hard contact.

When a football running back uses the term, it means that as soon as he takes the handoff, he has an unmistakable feel for where his blockers are positioned, where the pressure will be coming from and what he must do to run to daylight.

In 1991, I was "in the zone" the way few jockeys have ever been. I had always thought I was good and, admittedly, acted as though I was better than I really was at the time. But now, my heart told me I could be great—and my mind believed it. And it was all because I had beaten the bottle.

I am firmly convinced that if I had not hit bottom, I would never have been able to see my way to the top.

The owners and trainers were beginning to believe in me, too. My narrow triumph with Proper Reality in the 1989 Metropolitan Handicap and then with Home at Last in the Super Derby in 1990 had made them all sit up and take notice.

There are riders who thrive on premier races. They can always be counted on to give their mount the best possible chance when millions of dollars in purses and breeding value are on the line. And there are those who, deep down, shrink from pressure and are better suited to cheap claiming races. More and more, I was being viewed as a go-to rider when the stakes were high—and the stakes were certainly high in 1991.

When I reflect on my transformation from nonchalant "two-o'clock jock" to champion rider, it is fitting that the horse who played such a huge role in that process was one with a fairy-tale name: Hansel. I received the opportunity to ride him unexpectedly when, in the run-up to the $500,000 Jim Beam Stakes, a major stepping-stone for three-year-olds at Kentucky's Turfway Park, his regular jockey, Pat Day, had a conflict and chose a horse named Richman instead.

Jockeys and their agents are faced with these kinds of decisions on a regular basis. It is particularly difficult when they're trying to assess three-year-olds because these horses mature, mentally and physically, at wildly differing rates. Some horses are simply more precocious than others, while others get better with time. Some horses look like they're going to set the world on fire and then fizzle out, while undistinguished counterparts blossom into champions.

In this case, Pat made the wrong call, as we all have done many times. Hansel whipped second-place Richman by two and a quarter lengths and blazed the 1⅛ miles in 1:46⅗ seconds, demolishing the track record.

That positioned Hansel as the horse to beat in the Kentucky Derby. I am sure Day and his agent used all of their powers of persuasion to try to regain the mount, and to this day I am appreciative that owner Joe Allbritton and trainer Frank Brothers stuck with me instead of going back to Pat, whose résumé was certainly more impressive than mine at that point.

I was extremely eager to reward them on that first Saturday in May, and I was convinced I had the horsepower to do it. Hansel had been nothing short of brilliant in his prep race, and I could feel the eyes of the racing world—and their dollars—on us the minute we stepped onto the Churchill Downs track. We went off as the 5 to 2 favorite.

As we passed in the post parade beneath the shadows of the twin spires, however, I must admit that alarms began to sound. There was no bounce to Hansel's step. When he warmed up, he was dull. I'd already had concerns because I knew my colt could be intimidated if forced to run inside—the clods of dirt flying back at him tended to discourage him—and we were running from the sixth post. It was imperative that he be placed outside, no mean feat in a congested field of sixteen.

I hoped he would brighten when we entered the starting gate, and his adrenaline did seem to kick in at the start. But in his first few strides, I could tell he lacked punch. I stayed patient, hoping he would find a much higher gear in the backstretch, but it wasn't happening. I made sure to steer Hansel outside. No difference.

Strike the Gold won. We were no better than tenth.

The chart of the 117th Kentucky Derby tells the story: "Hansel, well placed while five wide into the backstretch, remained within easy striking distance for a mile and ducked in while tiring."

On what should have been the most important day of my career so far, my colt was a no-show. I had done my job, and there was some consolation in that. But after beginning the day with such high expectations, tenth place was a dreadful disappointment.

How was it that Hansel, so powerful only the start before, had come up so empty?

The vast majority of the time, a trainer can pinpoint the reason for a bad performance. Often, it's medical. The veterinarian uses an arthroscope to check the horse's lungs, and may find a buildup of mucus, a sign of infection or evidence of bleeding. Other times, a horse develops inflammation in a knee or ankle, indicating that that area has been troubling him. Trainers want to know. There is nothing more exasperating than operating blindly.

Frank Brothers was no different. He explored all those avenues, and many more besides—and came up with nothing. Zero. No reason at all why the most promising horse ever to enter his barn had fallen so short of great expectations.

This was the only certainty: On the most important day of his life, Hansel had thrown in a clunker.

"I've run a lot of beaten favorites, and eighty or ninety percent of them you understand why they run bad," Frank told the media. "This was one of that other ten or twenty percent. I couldn't come up with a single excuse. For whatever reason, he didn't fire. I was as low as a trainer could get."

Since he could find no explanation, the most pressing question became what he should do next. The Preakness was only two weeks away, and that just seemed too soon, given Hansel's performance, so instead Frank brought Hansel back to his home base at Arlington International Racecourse, near Chicago. He thought he would give Hansel some time and point him toward the Arlington Classic. Let the others contest the rest of the Triple Crown.

But when Hansel recognized Arlington's familiar surroundings, it was as if he had risen from the dead. Handlers can tell how their horses are feeling by their appetite at feeding time, the way they train, their level of alertness when approached. As listless as Hansel had been in Kentucky, now he was a handful.

I was mowing my lawn on Tuesday of Preakness week when Suzee approached, cordless phone in hand. It was an urgent call from my agent, Bob Frieze. Hansel had torn through a three-furlong workout at Arlington in 34⅗ seconds. Drop everything, I was told. We were headed to Baltimore!

The decision came so late there wasn't even time to make flight arrangements for Hansel. He had to be vanned from Illinois to Maryland.

"I thought of a hundred reasons to come and a hundred reasons not to come," Frank would say later of the decision he made jointly with Allbritton. "We went for the gusto."

And so did I. Still, I approached my second Preakness—I had run third in 1982 aboard Cut Away—with equal amounts of excitement and trepidation. I had experienced both ends of the spectrum with Hansel. Which horse would show?

Trainers do whatever they can to fill their riders with confidence, and Frank did that, assuring me that the sizzling workout was only one sign of how well Hansel had been training. I decided we'd just have to test it. In the race, I'd prompt him and make sure he was in the thick of the fight early, then see how many punches he would throw after that.

That Saturday, Hansel broke well, and I gently coaxed him into position a few lengths off the early leaders. I could tell he was back on top of his game by the way he barreled around the first turn. To my delight, he was extremely aggressive. While I was worried about moving too soon, his recent history told me I should not signal him to stop if he wanted to go, so I let him run.

He put away Olympio, the talented horse who was running in second, with startling ease. Then he headed Corporate Report six furlongs into the 1¾6-mile race. His ears were pricked to blow by. Decision time. I was either going to play the role of the fool for making the lead too soon or the 116th Preakness was about to become ours. Well, what else were we here for? I let him out a notch. He opened a four-length advantage. I cracked him once with the whip. Five lengths. Another lash. Six lengths.

I was going to win the Preakness!

After having to rely on my father to line up my first mounts because no agent believed in me, after calling a can of soup a hot meal my first summer away from home, after so many drunken nights and too few successful days, I was about to score my first victory in a Triple Crown race.

Hansel blew away Corporate Report by seven lengths. Derby champ Strike the Gold was never a factor, finishing sixth in a field of eight. In fact, after studying the television replay, I realized that I had never even needed to lay a finger on my horse. He'd been prepared to do it all by himself as long as I was a willing passenger.

But in truth, I had not been hitting Hansel to urge him to finish the job. I'd been hitting him for my own sake. Emotions, and inexperience in Triple Crown races, had gotten the best of me. A hand ride would have done just fine and allowed me to reserve more for the grueling 1½-mile Belmont Stakes. As my career advanced, I learned to look at the three-races-in-five-weeks grind as a whole. If there was a chance to spare any effort at all, it had to be done.

I was hardly alone in my mistake. Many riders have allowed their mounts to win the Preakness by far larger margins than necessary—and paid for it later.

In 2003, Funny Cide had an easy lead in the Preakness. He could have coasted. Instead, his jockey allowed Funny Cide to win by nine and three-quarter lengths. Exhilarating, sure—but did it take too much out of the horse? Barclay Tagg, Funny Cide's trainer, still thinks his colt's third-place Belmont finish, and his failure to become a Triple Crown champion, was due to that stretch drive. Personally, I think that was a factor, but there were plenty of other reasons as well.

I should know. I was on Empire Maker, the horse that beat Funny Cide in the Belmont Stakes—and he was just a better horse. He had already shown it when he defeated Funny Cide by half a length in the Wood Memorial, their Derby prep race. Empire Maker toyed with him that day. He could have won by much more if I had just asked him to.

Beyond that, Funny Cide was the son of a sprinter, Distorted Humor, and simply lacked the breeding to last the mile and a half. And any slim chance he might have had was eliminated that week when crackling workouts put him too much on edge for the marathon distance. After that final work, I predicted he would run like a rank horse who could not be controlled—and that's exactly what happened.

Then there was 2004, the year of Smarty Jones. Once again, a horse won the first two legs, and once again, his jockey did not conserve him for the Belmont. Instead, he let Smarty Jones win the Preakness by an unprecedented eleven and a half lengths.

In the Belmont, some say my own assertive early handling of my horse Eddington was meant to act as a spoiler, to wear Smarty Jones down, but anyone who thinks I was intent on spoiling the Smarty Party is way off-base. I ride to win, never to beat another horse, and that is exactly what I did with Eddington.

Trainer Mark Hennig and I had worked on Eddington's focus throughout the spring, because the horse had continually failed to put it all together. Mark put a very sharp work into him before the Belmont because our plan was to have him on the engine right away. We wanted him to know he was in a race the minute he left the gate. We hoped and believed that would keep him from becoming distracted the way he had before.

We had told anybody who would listen that we would put him in the game from the beginning, and that is exactly what we did. If the jockey was paying any attention, he knew early pressure was going to come from me. Rock Hard Ten joined the fray as well.

There are no gifts in racing. Everything must be earned, especially Triple Crowns. In the end, Edgar Prado rallied Birdstone to a one-length victory over Smarty Jones in the final leg. He even apologized, because he genuinely felt awful about depriving the

Age three, riding the family's first horse, a Shetland pony named Lady. *(Bailey family)*

At eight, with my sisters Becky (left) and Kathy (right), and our parents, James and Betty. *(Bailey family)*

My second professional mount, at Sunland Park, New Mexico, 1974. Note the long hair. *(Bailey family)*

The Kentucky Derby:
winning with Sea Hero
in 1993. (*Copyright © 2004
by Barbara D. Livingston*)

Rounding the turn with
Grindstone, 1996 Kentucky Derby
(*Horsephotos/Michael J. Marten*)

. . . and celebrating the photo-finish victory.
(*Jan Perret*)

The immortal Cigar: the $1,050,000 Arlington Citation Challenge, 1996.
(Jeff Coady, Full Stride Productions, Inc.)

In the winner's circle with Tina Mott and Suzee after Cigar's victory
in the 1995 Breeders' Cup Classic. *(Bailey family)*

Visiting Cigar
at Bill Mott's barn.
(Horsephotos / Michael J. Marten)

Visiting Cigar in retirement at
Kentucky Horse Park, 2004.
(Elizabeth Ann Holzback)

Riding Red Bullet to victory over Fusaichi Pegasus
in the 2000 Preakness. *(AP / Wide World Photos)*

Celebrating aboard Empire Maker
after winning the 2003 Belmont
Stakes (and denying Funny Cide the
Triple Crown). *(AP / Wide World Photos)*

Two great horses: Skip Away during a public workout

(Copyright © 2004 by Barbara D. Livingston)

. . . and Medaglia d'Oro in the winner's circle at the 2002 Travers,
Saratoga, New York. *(Horsephotos / Tamara Faulkner)*

It's a thrill to win honors—but they'd be nothing without my family. With Suzee and Justin at the Hall of Fame induction, 1995. *(Bailey family)*

With Justin, receiving the Eclipse Award for jockey of the year, 2001, one of seven I received between 1995 and 2003. *(Horsephotos / Joseph DiOrio)*

Justin and me in the New York Yankees dugout, 2001, with Don Zimmer and Derek Jeter. *(New York Yankees / Mark Mandrake)*

It's been an exhilarating ride.

(Horsephotos / Erik Hjermstad)

Thank you all.

(Copyright © 2004 by Barbara D. Livingston)

sport of a much-needed superstar. But he was only doing his job, and so was I.

Many great horses and jockeys have come to Belmont to participate in the third long leg of the Triple Crown and been duped into moving prematurely. It has always seemed odd to me that jockeys unfamiliar with this long-distance race on this huge track don't ride several days prior in order to get a feel of the size, distance and shape of Belmont Park.

BACK TO 1991 AND HANSEL, HOWEVER. I WAS REGRETting my own loss of cool in the Preakness. During the long three weeks before the Belmont, all I could wonder was: Had I enough left in the tank?

The last jewel of the Triple Crown is known as the "Test of a Champion" for many reasons, not the least of which is the vast amount of ground these youngsters are asked to cover. The mile-and-a-half challenge is something they will never be asked to meet again. The distance is the ultimate measure of breeding and heart. After Hansel's lifeless Derby and his hard trip in the Preakness, I was not sure where he stood on either count.

On Belmont day, he warmed up well and left the gate in good order. With every step, I was thinking I had to make this as easy on him as possible. No stops and starts. No wasted motion. No false moves.

I kept him well out on the track and allowed him to settle into an easy rhythm behind the early leaders. Not surprisingly, Corporate Report and Pat Day were showing the way through the opening half-mile. Hansel moved to Corporate Report's throat latch with five furlongs remaining.

We were far from the roaring crowd on the vast Belmont oval. As odd as this may sound, I was struck by the relative stillness of the moment. There was the labored breathing of horses, the pounding of hoofs, and that was all. I felt an urge to share this thought with someone. Pat was the only one around.

"Sure is quiet here," I called across to him.

Pat stared ahead, consumed by his thoughts. He never said a word.

Maybe the remark was my way of taking a breather from the tension. I was trying to keep Hansel in cruise control for as long as possible. I knew we could leave Corporate Report behind whenever we chose. The greatest obstacle to victory, at that point, was our ability to nurse his speed through the exhausting distance.

When did I want to let him out and try to steal away?

I was tormented by the memory of the legion of riders who had cost themselves with a premature move. Hansel would be the hero if we won. I sure as hell did not want to be the goat if we lost.

As soon as we straightened for home, I asked Hansel for his absolute life. His courage and stamina would never again be tested as they were now. The "heart" question was soon answered as he edged away in the upper stretch—but then his breeding and stamina began to fail him. He started to drift out.

Strike the Gold, so disappointing in the Preakness, was hell-bent on atonement. He was coming at us hard, roaring down the lane, just as I had expected he would. I worked feverishly on Hansel's right side, trying to keep him on the straight and narrow, straining to hold him together.

Where was the wire?

Hansel was absolutely rubber-legged in the final sixteenth of a mile. He was like a dazed boxer who sees the arena spinning, spinning as he fights to stand.

Where was the wire?

We were a couple of strides from home. Strike the Gold was gaining with every leap.

Where was the wire?

I pleaded with Hansel for something, anything—and he found it. By sheer willpower, he crossed the finish line first, by a diminishing head.

I was proud of Hansel, who was all heart, and proud of myself for riding a tremendous race. I had taken a calculated risk and had not allowed the fear of making a mistake to become an unwelcome passenger.

My gut had told me I would get the jump on Chris Antley by moving when I did, and that is exactly what happened. It made all the difference, with one million dollars in Triple Crown bonus money up for grabs.

It was a lesson I would always keep in mind from that point forward. My instinct served me almost without fail.

The journey with Hansel brought more than fame and fortune, by the way. It helped me and Suzee develop a lasting friendship with owner Joe Allbritton and his wife, Barbie, one that we will always cherish. After the Belmont, we were invited to a party they hosted at the Carlyle Hotel in Manhattan. I had been steadily declining invitations in my sobriety, and this was the first one I accepted. I did so with no trepidation whatsoever. When Joe lifted a glass of champagne for a toast, I raised a glass of water. I don't know if anyone even noticed the difference.

Through the years, Joe, who owns several banks among other businesses, would offer invaluable financial advice, and the night Justin was born, the door to Suzee's hospital room opened slowly and there was Barbie to share our joy. In a what-have-you-done-for-me-lately world marked by fleeting relationships, Joe and Barbie are the real deal. They are forever giving of their friendship.

And there was more. My first Belmont was not my only triumph—in fact, it was the centerpiece of an unbelievable weekend. On the undercard, I had ridden Fly So Free from well off the pace to a rousing two-length score in the seven-furlong Riva Ridge. Then Sunday, in the 1⅛-mile Mother Goose, I made sure Meadow Star got an immediate jump on Lite Light, then held her off by a nostril in my second photo finish in as many afternoons.

That made it three horses with different running styles winning at different distances. It was treated as major news when I piloted each of them flawlessly. "Bailey's Personal Triple Crown," read a headline in *The New York Times*.

"I've been riding seventeen years, but I don't understand the scope of what happened to me," I said in an interview as soon as the whirlwind was over.

It soon became clear. Those back-to-back-to-back master-pieces worked wonders for my business. I suddenly had a choice of horses in major stakes. No more visiting barns and pleading for mounts.

To give just one example, there is no doubt in my mind that my success in the spring led to my grand opportunity in the fall. I was mowing the lawn—once again—when Suzee came out, phone in hand. I now had a mount in the $3 million Breeders'

Cup Classic, and not just any horse; I was set to ride Black Tie Affair, a Horse of the Year candidate who had already won four consecutive starts.

Speed horse Farma Way had dropped out due to injury, so Black Tie Affair loomed as the primary speed in the $1\frac{1}{4}$-mile Classic at Churchill Downs, along with Twilight Agenda. I decided I would be more than happy to lay second if Chris McCarron and Twilight Agenda wanted the lead.

I always viewed my ability to plot out a race as one of my greatest assets, along with the intelligence and decisiveness to make immediate adjustments. Both came into play that afternoon.

When I looked for Twilight Agenda after the first jump, he was nowhere to be found, so I immediately dropped over to the rail and seized control. Black Tie Affair completed the opening quarter of a mile in a comfortable $24\frac{1}{5}$ seconds. He was very much in hand through an opening half-mile in $48\frac{2}{5}$. Still alone on the lead. The first three-quarters of a mile went in $1{:}12\frac{3}{5}$. My smile was growing wider with every fraction.

The reason I hadn't found Twilight Agenda was that he had bobbled at the start, and although I glanced back now and saw he was gaining, my smile stayed in place. I had not yet asked my horse for anything. When I did, it was over. His one-and-a-quarter-length decision, in $2{:}02\frac{4}{5}$ seconds, was about the easiest victory in a $3 million race you would ever want to see. He did indeed secure Horse of the Year honors, as well as Champion Older Male.

As for me, well, a fairy-tale year was over. I was indebted to Hansel, who bent but did not break, and to Fly So Free, Meadow Star and Black Tie Affair. As I entered the Breeders' Cup winner's circle for the first time, I knew I would never have been there without Suzee's unfailing love.

"Enjoy the moment! Enjoy the moment!" she kept telling me.

Finally, I was able to do that. There was no urge to rush off to celebrate with vodka and orange juice, my old but false friends. My breakthrough season, and newfound marital happiness, reaffirmed the value of sobriety.

While I will always be an alcoholic, I felt I was on firm ground in my recovery. That, of course, was the most significant victory of all in unforgettable 1991.

I entered 1992 with all kinds of momentum. I topped the standings at Keeneland's spring meeting and continued to ride well in the summer and fall. I swept three stakes races on the inaugural Breeders' Cup Preview Day at Belmont Park, prevailing with Sea Hero in the Champagne Stakes, Shared Interest in the First Flight Handicap and Educated Risk in the Frizette.

Thoughts of the Champagne stayed with me throughout the winter, for in that event for two-year-olds Sea Hero displayed exceptional quality. With maturity, it was easy to envision him as a Kentucky Derby champion—and I still hadn't won a Derby. But that would have to wait. There was still one more adventure left in 1993, and it represented the most improbable victory of my career. Actually, it represents the most improbable Breeders' Cup victory in any jockey's career.

Arcangues was a French horse ridden by Mike Smith, but when trainer H. Allen Jerkens decided to enter Devil His Due in the Classic and offered it to him, Smith made the obvious decision. Arcangues had many factors against him.

The journey, for one thing. The Breeders' Cup was at Santa Anita in Arcadia, California, that year, and that kind of trip has some foreign equine athletes beaten the minute they touch down. Arcangues had also never run outside France, and beyond that, he was a turf specialist being asked to leave his preferred surface for the first time in sixteen career starts to oppose the best dirt horses in the world. Who would choose him?

I agreed to ride Arcangues simply because it beat the alternative—which was to watch the race in the jocks' room. I had already rejected a number of horses, thinking something better would come along. Nothing had, and I was flattered that the horse's connections seemed to want me badly.

"When you run in these big American races, you need a top American jockey," Alec Wildenstein, son of owner Daniel Wildenstein, told the media. "That's why we went after Mr. Bailey."

From my standpoint, it was a shot at a three-million-dollar purse, even if it was a tremendous long shot, and so I would give it my best. Once it was clear Arcangues did not belong, I would make sure we got the heck out of the way. On paper, this edition of the Classic appeared to have trainer Bobby Frankel's name written all over it. He was fully armed with a burner in Bertrando, another speedster in Marquetry and the solid Missionary Ridge.

When I went to the paddock to get a leg up on Arcangues, I knew next to nothing about him other than his post position, which was 12. Was he a bay or a gray? No idea. Could not even pronounce his name. I assumed his trainer, Andre Fabre, would provide thorough instructions as to the five-year-old's wants and needs, but Andre was initially nowhere to be found.

Arcangues, it turned out, was a gorgeous chestnut who was accompanied by a lad on either side. They saw me and started gesturing and talking excitedly. No use. This Texan does not speak a word of French. By the time Andre ran up, the crowd noise had risen. I could not make out a word he said.

I would have to improvise. Most European horses are trained to relax and drop back in the pack before they uncork one sustained run. That game plan made as much sense as any, so I decided to try it.

I glanced at the tote board during the post parade. Ninety-nine to one! If I had had the option of hopping off just then, I probably would have. I did not want to finish twenty lengths behind and embarrass myself, and that seemed like a distinct possibility. Some days chicken, some days feathers. Sure felt like a feathers day.

I really did not know much about Andre at the time. If I had, I would have understood that he was too good a conditioner to fly a horse from one continent to another for no reason. I was also unaware that Arcangues had floundered on some of Europe's undulating turf courses due to a disk problem in his back, that he had worked exceptionally well on dirt the last two months and that he might relish the move to Santa Anita's hard and fast dirt strip.

Arcangues warmed up well, which is not always the case with European imports. That told me he had handled the trip just fine. One obstacle gone. Another concern was eliminated when, after he broke from well outside, he was able to work into a good position near the rail as we hit the first turn. He was happy as could be running on dirt.

He was already showing me enough that I knew he would not finish last. That was a relief. I never wanted to look bad, especially before an international audience on Breeders' Cup Day. I would give Arcangues the most ground-saving trip possible.

Maybe we could cut ourselves a slice of that three-million-dollar pie after all.

The beauty of this race for me was that there was absolutely no pressure. Few binoculars were riveted on me. Other riders were not shooting for me. I was an afterthought, if that.

I allowed Arcangues to do as he pleased. He was a leisurely tenth through the opening half. Bertrando, as expected, hummed along in front. I was not thinking about him at all.

Arcangues was telling me he was ready to pick it up. I looked for a live horse we might attempt to follow toward the first flight.

The trailblazer for us turned out to be Ezzoud, another foreign entry with seemingly impossible odds. He was 105–1. The bettors' skepticism did not matter at that point. He was moving along well, which was all I wanted, and now so was I.

Midway through the final turn, I knew I would not be going home with empty pockets. We were perfectly positioned inside. We were going to get a piece. But how big a piece?

Ezzoud was starting to run to dismal expectations and calling it a day. Arcangues had something left. Given my unfamiliarity with him, I had no idea how much. Then we found a seam that allowed me to split Kissin Kris, who had rallied into striking position, and Marquetry, whose energy was flagging. Arcangues squeezed through those two.

My God! I thought. *I might have a chance to win!*

We had only Gary Stevens and Bertrando to catch. Arcangues gave me a tremendous burst.

"I thought the race was over and here comes this horse," Stevens would say later, "and I have no idea who he is."

At the end, my no-hoper made it look easy. He was two lengths to the good, with Bertrando second best.

While I rarely wager and it had never even remotely entered my mind to risk a dollar on my mount, I could not help but look over for the payoffs. My jaw dropped. We were paying $269.20 for a $2 wager to win, an unheard-of return for a Breeders' Cup race!

The name is pronounced Ar-KONG. As in King Kong.

Nine

COMING UP ROSES

I am a realist, not a dreamer.

When I learned to ride as a boy, when I exercised Thoroughbreds at dawn as a teenager, when I rode as an adult early in my career, I was not driven by the thought of winning the Kentucky Derby. It was a huge race, probably too big for me. I doubted I would ever be part of one.

That thought did not particularly bother me. It certainly did not keep me up on those evenings when alcohol turned out my lights. If I ever made it to the most important race in the world, fine. If not, there were other races, lesser races, that were realistic goals and not a far-fetched dream.

Frankly, I was not all that excited after I worked up to my first Derby mount, New Discovery, in 1982. I studied his past performances and those of the rest of the field, looking for a ray of hope, and could not find one. I kept telling myself that anything can and does happen in racing, and tried to hang on to that as hard as I could.

It helped my confidence when I won the Twin Spires aboard Cut Away as part of the undercard. Then it was time for my first Derby.

My God!

As I described before, there is nothing to prepare you for the experience of stepping onto that track. My body shivered with excitement.

As I gazed at the teeming grandstand, as I smiled at the bedlam in the infield, I understood that the Derby is so much more than a horse race. It epitomizes the American Dream, offering hope that enough sweat can allow anyone to smell the roses. With the joyful mayhem it compresses into two minutes and change, the Derby affirms life itself.

To see more than a hundred thousand fans sway to the strains of "My Old Kentucky Home," to listen to the power of the words and music Stephen Foster wrote in 1853, is to be grateful for every sunrise, every breath.

Weep no more, my lady,
Oh weep no more today!
We will sing one song for the old Kentucky home,
For the old Kentucky home far away.

I was choked up. I thought of my mother, Betty, and how dutifully she had listened to my races even as cancer ravaged her body. I thought of my father, Jim, and the blows he had absorbed to maintain his college boxing scholarship and advance himself and ultimately his children. I thought of my boyhood, when I was never quite big enough or tall enough to play.

The power of my first Derby experience turned this hardened realist into a dreamer.

New Discovery was every bit as overmatched as I feared he would be. He was unable to keep up the first time we passed the stands. It never got any better after that. That last half-mile seemed as though it took forever, and it nearly did. We were eighteenth of nineteen.

Yet New Discovery was aptly named for my debut. I discovered that day what the Derby is all about. More than that, I began to dream that I could win one. It is called Derby Fever.

As I tried and failed with Conquistarose (ninth, 1987), Proper Reality (fourth, 1988), Hansel (tenth, 1991) and Technology (tenth, 1992), my symptoms worsened. I did not just want to win the Derby. If my career was to matter, I felt I had to win one.

People you meet have two questions once they know you are a jockey.

"Have you ever ridden in the Derby?"

Once they know that you have, the second question is automatic.

"Ever win one?"

I could not live with that "no" hanging out there.

With each attempt, my confidence grew. The Derby did not rattle me. Once the emotions inevitably stirred by the playing of "My Old Kentucky Home" had passed, I understood exactly what needed to be done.

Winning requires luck as much as greatness. The horse must be good enough. The jockey must be cool enough. Then everything must break your way.

Since the 1¼-mile classic is always a cavalry charge, with the field at or near the maximum of twenty starters based on graded stakes earnings, positioning entering and leaving the first turn is huge. You want to get there with as little jostling, as little contact, as possible. There were times when I gladly sacrificed placement to avoid a bumping match. While the Run for the Roses cannot be won at the first turn, I have seen countless dreams die there.

The Derby champion is often the three-year-old who can adjust his running style due to intense crowding, then pass battered opponents toward the end. Think mid-Manhattan subway during rush hour, wearing a backpack. That is an exhausting experience, one to be avoided at all costs. It is the same for young horses who get the worst of it in the Derby. Position in the first flight, if it comes at a price, is never worth it.

Some say traffic should be reduced by being more selective about which horses are eligible to start. As much as I do not like seeing improbable long shots clutter the Derby, I do not agree. If I owned a Thoroughbred who had any hope at all, you had better believe I would want to take that shot, knowing it may never come around again.

There are riders who spend so much time complaining about Derby conditions that it saps their mental energy. The unpredictability that the congested field helps to create is part of racing lore. Deal with it!

By the time Sea Hero flashed his brilliance by winning the Champagne Stakes for me in 1992, I was gripped by Derby

Fever. I had felt what it would be like to win when Proper Reality briefly held second as we turned for home in 1988. The roar of that crowd—the "Wall of Sound," as it is called—was still ringing in my ears.

I fed off that race because I knew I had handled Proper Reality perfectly and been impervious to my surroundings. If the pressure of that Derby could not rattle me, I knew no race ever could. I always kept my composure from that point forward, and that was the primary reason for my growing reputation as a money rider.

I felt certain I could get the job done if the right horse came along. Sea Hero sure looked to be that horse. He was put together well; his lineage was impeccable.

The bay son of Polish Navy had been bred in Virginia by Paul Mellon. That alone reassured me he would be able to answer the biggest question of all on the first Saturday in May. He would handle the mile and a quarter. All of Mr. Mellon's horses were intended for the classic distance. With Mack Miller as the trainer, I knew everything possible would be done to have the colt at his best for the Triple Crown series.

My high hopes dimmed when Sea Hero, perfectly positioned for a big run in the Breeders' Cup Juvenile at Gulfstream Park in Florida at the end of October, did not fire at all. On an afternoon when he was no more than mediocre, he got exactly what he deserved. He finished seventh of thirteen.

More disappointment came early in 1993. Sea Hero was neither training well nor acting well. And it showed. He ran a disappointing fourth in the Palm Beach Stakes at Gulfstream. Mack decided to pull him out of Florida and brought him back to Kentucky to regroup.

Mack also was starting to think Sea Hero belonged on grass. Mr. Mellon would have none of that. He was eighty-five years old. He had already started to disperse some of his stock as he made arrangements for an orderly transfer of his estate. He wanted one last stab at racing's ultimate prize.

As much as I wanted to see Mr. Mellon realize his lifelong dream, the realist in me was screaming that I had to find another Derby mount. I instructed my agent, Bob Frieze, to investigate every possible starter, to make every possible call.

Meanwhile, Mack was beseeching me not to give up on Sea Hero. He swore the colt was doing much better at his home base of Kentucky and thriving in the colder weather. Horses handle climates differently, just the way humans do. Sea Hero apparently had some polar bear in him.

At the same time, I know trainers tend to see what they want to see. Hope, after all, is what spurs them to check each stall at 5 A.M. day after day after day. Mack had sent out only one other Derby starter in his illustrious career, taking fifth with Jig Time in 1968. Mack was seventy-one. He heard the ticking of the clock just as loudly as Mr. Mellon.

As much as I respected Mack, I had to wonder if he was believing what he wanted to believe because the truth about his erratic colt was too crushing.

I nonetheless agreed to pilot Sea Hero in the Blue Grass Stakes, the race he would use to prep for the Derby. While I was braced for the worst, I came out of the Blue Grass optimistic again. After a troubled trip, he had closed steadily for fourth. And I had learned something that could make the difference at Churchill Downs.

It is uncommon for jockeys to recommend, and trainers to

consider, a change of equipment before their horse runs the most important race of his life. My relationship with Mack was such that I did not hesitate to suggest that Sea Hero might benefit from the removal of blinkers.

I was confident the colt would be aggressive and responsive without them. As I went over the Blue Grass time and time again, I kept thinking of repeated instances in which he had been reluctant to go through holes. If the blinkers came off, there was a decent chance that hesitation would disappear.

It was worth trying, and I knew something would have to change if we were to defeat deserving favorite Prairie Bayou. I all but pleaded with Mack to accept my recommendation. He took it under advisement.

I redoubled my efforts to land on a top contender and stepped up the pressure on Bob to make that happen. Try as he might, nothing was available. As unorthodox as it was, Mack agreed to experiment in the Derby. He would give Sea Hero an eyeful on Derby Day by running him without blinkers.

Sea Hero trained well and drew favorably, receiving post 6 of nineteen. I thought I would have a legitimate chance if I could get my inconsistent colt to relax early. We had not yet traveled a hundred yards before it was clear my recommendation had worked.

Sea Hero was sharp from the outset and almost immediately settled into a long, looping stride. The raucous crowd had not unnerved him. The tangle of horses who had rushed in front of us was not intimidating him.

He was in his own little world, and I was in mine. It was a beautiful place. It was as if we were in our own bubble, running between a flight of horses. I was accomplishing exactly what I wanted. We swept around the first turn without any jarring contact, without a hint of trouble, and I had not been forced to alter my horse's style to achieve that.

This could not be working out any better, I thought.

The fact that we were falling many lengths from the lead did not bother me. Sea Hero preferred to take his time early. I was prepared for a long, uphill climb. While the track was officially listed as fast, it was a bit moist as well. I had stacked six pairs of goggles so that I could almost always have clear vision.

The ability to observe what was happening many lengths in front of me would be vital to our success. If I saw a rider move his hand ever so slightly and his horse did not quicken his action, that was no horse to follow. If I noticed that a jockey placed his whip against his horse's side and got a spark in response, we would probably do well to stay close to him.

Picking the right rider to follow in any race is essential when you are assigned to a closer. I know different jockeys not by the colors of their silks but by their styles. No two people sit on a horse quite the same way. We all have tendencies that become predictable. I always prided myself on knowing my counterparts as well as they knew themselves.

Storm Tower, with Rick Wilson in the irons, took the big field through the opening three-quarters of a mile. His cheap speed did not faze me at all. Sea Hero, twelfth after the opening half-mile, was gaining momentum like an old steam locomotive on the backstretch. I went to work.

Every time we approached a wall of Thoroughbreds, some jockey would unwittingly make a move that opened a hole for me. Another flight, another crease. It was a constant measured progression. It was magical.

As we approached the final turn, we still had two groups in

front of us. I remained cool and calculating. Experience gained from five previous Derby failures taught me there would be ample opportunity at this juncture. Horses would be flagging. Horses would be stopping. Horses would be rallying.

We mounted our charge.

I thought of Mack's instructions, which were to come from off the pace and work my way around horses by going outside of them. He always possessed confidence that his starters were good enough to lose ground and still get the job done. His worst fear was getting shut off on the rail.

Pacesetting Storm Tower had long ago called it a day. Of the three horses lined across the track in front of us, two drifted out from fatigue. I had no choice but to cast Mack's wishes aside. I gratefully dropped inside with minimal effort.

Personal Hope, with Gary Stevens in the irons, was still ahead of us. Gary was asking for something that was not there.

We were about to make the lead!

This is almost too easy, I thought.

With the whip in my right hand, I rapped Sea Hero once, twice, three times. We slingshotted out of the final turn and unleashed an all-out drive along the rail. I feverishly worked his left side as he pulled away.

I hope Sea Hero can forgive my overzealousness. I could not take any chances. I had to be sure to keep his mind on the task. The dream was too real. The history too large.

Mike Smith had successfully roused Prairie Bayou. He was coming with too little too late. With an eighth of a mile to go, the conclusion was clear. I had saved more than enough for the end.

I am going to win the Kentucky Derby, I thought. *I am going to win the Kentucky Derby!*

We flashed across the wire two and a half lengths ahead of Prairie Bayou. Late-running Wild Gale blew in a head behind him.

I looked to the heavens and thanked God for so much more than a race result. Tears welled in my eyes.

SUZEE: *I sat at home in Long Island watching the telecast with my mom, Justin, and my two dogs. When he started to make his move splitting one group of horses after another, I knew everything was going his way and my heart started to beat faster.*

"Go, Jerry! Come on, Jerry! Come on, Jerry! Come on, Jerry!" I shouted over and over. The dogs began barking while little Justin looked on. Between my rooting and the barking dogs, we could barely hear the telecast as Sea Hero pounded home.

I screamed, then cried for joy. I was so proud of Jerry and thankful for that outcome. I briefly thought of all that we would have missed if the right choices had not been made.

I was a winner for reasons that had nothing to do with my horse finishing first in the only race that means something to casual fans. I was a winner in the most important sense of the word. In sobriety, I had become a good husband to Suzee, a good father to six-month-old Justin and a good person.

So many emotions surfaced. I was sad because my wife was not there. I was angry at myself for advising her to stay home with Justin because I feared Sea Hero was not good enough.

SUZEE: *Yes, I wished I was there with him, but Justin was much too young to be part of that massive crowd and chaotic scene. Amid all of the celebration and the interview requests, Jerry let me and Justin*

know how much he missed us and wished we were there with him.
The three of us would have our time to celebrate soon enough.

And I was thrilled for Mack, who had stuck with me in the end and now, in the twilight of his career, had claimed his greatest triumph.

MACK: *The horse broke from the number-six post position and was way back on the turn and way back on the backside. I nudged Mr. Mellon and said, "Paul, I don't feel very good right now."*

Going into the last turn, he took off and he went through the field. Jerry said after he got to the quarter pole, the Red Sea parted. After that, it was over.

Jerry never got confused, never got in a hurry. He bided his time, the way good riders are supposed to do.

When I went down to unsaddle the horse, Mr. Mellon said, "Mack, I have some tickets to cash. I think we'll need a Brinks truck."

Sea Hero went off at almost 13 to 1. Mr. Mellon collected $26,000 and distributed all of that money to his employees. My father was right when he said, "As you walk through life, you cannot get any whitewash on you if you don't rub against it."

I was overjoyed for Mr. Mellon. He had invested millions in Thoroughbred racing and now, so full of life at age eighty-five, held aloft one of the few trophies that had eluded him.

As I waited to be interviewed on national television, I asked the gracious host, Jim McKay, if it would be acceptable for me to say hello to Suzee.

"Jerry," he answered, "it's your day. You can say whatever you want."

I was supposed to handle a horse named Key Contender for Mack in the next race. He had already arranged for a backup rider so I could attend the post-Derby news conference. Mack must have had a pretty strong idea that Sea Hero, for all of his unpredictability, would be on his game when it counted most.

It seemed as though there were a million questions to answer. As I reflected on my headlong pursuit of another mount when I had the right horse all along, I could not help but think I was destined to win the 119th Kentucky Derby. I will always believe that I simply played the lead role in a script written long ago.

I was so grateful for the outcome that I asked Chrysler, which planned to present a car to the winning jockey, to donate the value of that vehicle to the Jockeys' Disabled Riders Fund. I had done the same thing after the Preakness in 1991, with the two donations totaling $48,000.

The need to help riders paralyzed in accidents has always been dear to my heart. With one snap of a Thoroughbred's toothpick-like leg, that could easily be me at the end of any given day. I have always believed there is no better way to deal with the issue than for jockeys to take care of those who can no longer take care of themselves.

Pat Day and Mike Smith were among the riders who also asked Chrysler to make donations in lieu of a vehicle for winning a Triple Crown race.

As soon as the news conference ended, I hurriedly showered and returned to my hotel so I could speak at length to Suzee. We reminisced about my tumultuous ride with Mack and how I had continued our morning get-togethers even after he fired me in the autumn of 1986 only to rehire me early in 1988. We spoke of how Sea Hero proved you can look for an answer that is right in front of you. We thrilled in how complete our lives had become.

Time to celebrate with a room-service chicken sandwich—and bottled water.

When I boarded the plane the next morning for the flight to New York, my fellow passengers treated me to a warm round of applause. Here was this five-foot-five man with an armful of roses the morning after the Derby, so it was not hard to figure out who I was and what had happened.

When I presented the roses to Suzee, who had Justin in tow, life never felt so complete.

SUZEE: *I couldn't believe he brought the winner's roses home for me and Justin. It seemed that we hugged forever at the airport, forming our personal winner's circle. Sometimes, I just wanted to freeze the moment.*

As much as I was tempted to take the day off, I really didn't feel I had the option. Jockeys have day-in, day-out obligations that must be kept. It was off to Belmont Park for that day's card. NFL players have the entire offseason to kick back after the Super Bowl. Baseball players warm themselves throughout the winter with World Series memories. Jockeys never have time to savor their victories, only to heal their wounds. There are always races to be ridden, each of them of great magnitude for the owner involved.

Life changes overnight when you win the Derby. Carl Nafzger likes to joke that he went from "Carl Who?" to "Mr. Nafzger." That is about right.

"Mr. Bailey" was suddenly in demand every minute of every day. You do everything you can to share your happiness with family members, but then there are "friends" you have not heard from in years. And there are so many requests for one-on-one interviews it is nearly impossible to satisfy them all.

It was difficult to concentrate on anything except the next leg of the Triple Crown. While Sea Hero worked better for the Preakness than he had for the Derby, I had my concerns the week before the 1$\frac{3}{16}$-mile race. I did not feel he was handling the Pimlico surface well.

I tried to put that concern out of my mind as I allowed Sea Hero to drop back early and find a comfortable stride. Once he had done that, he showed no interest in taking me into the race on a speed-favoring track.

I pushed on his neck a few times midway through the backstretch. He did not respond to my energy.

I slapped his shoulder with my open hand. Still nothing.

I cracked him once, then twice, with the whip. No use.

As elated as I was at the end of the Derby, that is how downcast I felt after Sea Hero ran a dull fifth to Prairie Bayou in the next leg. Worse than the result was the fate of Union City, trained by D. Wayne Lukas. The promising three-year-old broke down and had to be humanely destroyed.

When I returned home, there were no messages. "Friends" from long ago had vanished as quickly as they had appeared. Suzee tried to soften the defeat.

"At least we have our privacy back," she said.

Since a $1 million bonus was offered based on points earned during the Triple Crown series, there was never any doubt that we would try Sea Hero in the Belmont Stakes. I thought it was a good omen when it rained before the 1½-mile contest, causing the track to be downgraded from fast to good. My horse loved a wet track.

On this day, however, there was nothing that was going to make him happy. His competitive juices were not flowing, to say the least. As he plodded along in the middle of the pack, I looked around for Prairie Bayou. While Colonial Affair was well on his way toward making Julie Krone the first female rider to win a Triple Crown race, perhaps we could bring home the $1 million bonus if the Preakness champion finished far enough behind us.

Prairie Bayou was nowhere to be found. I learned after the race he had broken down on the backstretch and suffered fatal injuries. We received the $1 million bonus, with my share totaling the standard ten percent or $100,000, but given the grim circumstances, there was no smile when the check arrived.

Not long after the Triple Crown was over, there was a knock at my door. Mr. Mellon had sent a handsome bronze statue of Sea Hero. It took my breath away as I placed it on display in a revolving bookcase. An inscription on the oak base read: "To Jerry Bailey, without whose great jockeyship I would have never won the Kentucky Derby."

Nothing could remove the smile from my face that day.

The enigmatic Sea Hero went on to add the Travers to his Champagne and Kentucky Derby triumphs. I will say this for him—he could pick his spots.

You might think my Derby Fever was cured in 1993. Not at all. It only intensifies with success.

Nothing boosts a jockey's business more than winning the Derby. I enjoyed an array of options as I looked for the right mount in 1994, starting with Go for Gin. I rode him to a strong second-place finish for trainer Nick Zito in the Wood Memorial, trailing only Irgun.

Nick asked me to commit to Go for Gin and gave me a reasonable amount of time to decide. When I had an opportunity to jump to Irgun, I did not hesitate. The next day, I was told Irgun had bruised his foot.

I quickly went back to Nick. Too late. He had already hired Chris McCarron. Irgun never made it to the starting gate. I wound up on Blumin Affair, a live long shot but a long shot nonetheless. Although my youngster closed powerfully for third, Go for Gin had made an easy lead on a sloppy track. There was no catching him. All I could do was stare ruefully at his hindquarters.

"There goes the horse I took off of," I muttered.

I was determined to make a good decision in 1995. D. Wayne Lukas called my agent, Bob Frieze, and offered us Thunder Gulch. The colt had finished a distant fourth in the Blue Grass. Lukas, however, expressed confidence that our combined talents could move him up. I was not so sure.

"That horse got beaten a long way," I told Bob. "Let's look for something else."

Something else turned out to be Tejano Run. Not a bad choice, because he made a late rush for second. But a terrible choice when you consider that I had refused the winner, Thunder Gulch.

I was furious, not at Bob but at myself. Yes, my agent had influenced my decisions. But the final call rested with me. And wrong calls had kept me from what easily could have been a three-race Derby winning streak.

When D. Wayne phoned early in 1996 to see if he could interest me in Grindstone, I was all cars. As he had shown so dramatically the spring before, Lukas knows how to have a three-year-old at his absolute best on the first Saturday in May.

He had picked out the Louisiana Derby as a key stop for Grindstone on the road to Kentucky. The son of 1990 Kentucky Derby champ Unbridled closed powerfully to win that prep race. He handled the task with ease.

My skin was hot to the touch again. Derby Fever.

That did not diminish when Grindstone placed second in the Arkansas Derby, his last stop before Churchill Downs. The winner had gotten loose on the lead, and I knew my mount had a difficult task from post 12. We had our sights set on a different Derby, anyway.

On to Kentucky.

Suzee was trying to decide whether to come or stay at home with Justin, who was still too young to be exposed to the Derby Day crush.

"Well, I've got some kind of chance," I said.

That was all she needed to hear.

"I'll be there," she promised.

The paddock scene was frenetic. An incredible five of the nineteen starters came from D. Wayne's barn. In addition to Grindstone, Prince of Thieves (Pat Day), Editor's Note (Gary Stevens), Victory Speech (Jose Santos) and Honour and Glory (Aaron Gryder) all required his attention.

We had held a team meeting back at the barn. D. Wayne emphasized that each of us was to do his best for the disparate ownership interests. He did not want a situation, however, where one of his horses engaged another to the ruination of both.

Grindstone was owned by the late William T. Young, then seventy-eight years young, who had made his fortune in peanut butter. He was as excited as a child on Christmas Day when the saddle cloth was slipped onto his dark bay colt and the buzzing crowd awaited the playing of "My Old Kentucky Home."

"If I win, golly Moses, send me to heaven!" he exclaimed.

If fate was smiling on Mr. Young, it did not show in the post position draw. We would load well out from the rail into number 15.

While Grindstone broke in good order, he did not show the same aggressiveness as he had in Louisiana. He did not want to assert himself, at least not yet. He was slipping farther and farther off the pace set by Honour and Glory, who had spurted to the front. At the same time, I had found my trouble-free bubble, just as I had with Sea Hero.

Knowing that Grindstone's style was to launch a prolonged rally, I had stacked five pairs of goggles, sacrificing peripheral vision to make sure I could spot everything that occurred in the first flight. Honour and Glory was humming along at a crisp pace with Matty G clinging to him in second.

Honour and Glory, with Gryder as an unhappy passenger, threw down an opening quarter of 22⅕ seconds, then zipped through one half of a mile in 46 seconds flat. When he sprinted the first six furlongs in 1:10, those were impossible fractions. He would soon be done.

Grindstone would have to pick it up to take advantage of the hot pace. I flipped down a new pair of goggles and chirped to him as we straightened out on the backside. He was willing.

As we accelerated, I looked for a horse to follow. I spotted Prince of Thieves, still under a snug hold from Pat Day. Following

Pat is not without risk. He is notorious for waiting until the last possible instant to move. He makes Job look impatient.

Still, Pat is a heady rider who knows how to carve out a clean trip. I would take my cue from him until the quarter pole, then figure it out from there.

Grindstone, fourteenth through the first three-quarters, began working his way toward the top as I changed goggles again. Honour and Glory had given way suddenly. Mattty G was stopping. Built for Pleasure, who had shown early life, was lifeless. It was the same for Semoran and Skip Away. Slightly built Grindstone, the smallest three-year-old in the race, continued his dogged advance.

We pushed inside to work our way past a tangle of horses, then angled out five wide entering the stretch. Cavonnier and Chris McCarron had taken over the lead, followed by Unbridled's Song and Halo Sunshine.

So much to do and so little time.

I yanked down my next-to-last set of goggles and pulled the trigger on Grindstone, smacking him on his right flank with the whip. He lowered his head and exploded.

I lashed him again on his right side. We picked off Halo Sunshine. I stung him once more. Unbridled's Song, wearing two bar shoes, was not fit for the challenge. I saw his rear end wobble a little, a telltale sign of a horse in distress. We roared past.

Cavonnier remained.

Was there enough time?

In an instant, I switched the whip to my left hand. I strained to see through eyewear that contained a film of dirt. No time to reach for my last pair. The used goggles dangled in front of my mouth, hindering my breathing. No time to shove them aside. We were flying at Cavonnier.

Was there enough time?

I pushed frantically on Grindstone's neck and whipped him just as furiously. He surged with every blow. We were at Cavonnier's flank.

Was there enough time?

We were at his throat. I struggled for air. My arms and legs burned with fatigue. The wire approached. One last surge. Grindstone and Cavonnier crossed together.

As we galloped out, I looked over at Chris.

"Who do you think won?"

He shook his head. "Too close to call."

An outrider approached me. "Did you win?" he asked.

"The only thing I know," I said, kicking my feet out of the irons, "is that I need to rest a minute before we go back."

I desperately wanted to win. I believed I deserved to win. I know this may sound cocky, but it comes from the heart. I felt no other rider of my era could have ridden Grindstone as well as I had just ridden him. In all the years I have had to reflect on it, there is not one thing I would have done differently.

At the time, though, I did not know if perfection was enough. The wait for results of the photo seemed interminable. I said a silent prayer.

"God, please let it be me."

It was!

My second Derby!

The first had been overwhelming. When I think of the moments immediately after that race, so much of it was a blur. This time, I made sure I soaked it all in. As we received an enormous round of applause on our way back toward the finish line, I looked at every section of the grandstand. I burned everything I could into my memory: the smiling faces, the outstretched hands, the magnificence of the roses.

And, of course, Suzee's presence made everything complete. I made sure not to enter the winner's circle until she had time to reach the enclosure. Little Grindstone needed time, anyway. He had laid his body out and was gasping for air.

SUZEE: *To win one Derby in a lifetime is a dream come true. To win two in a span of four years? It was just an unbelievable feeling and I was so grateful I could be there with Jerry. Winning a Derby is a miraculous moment that loses nothing in repeating.*

I wish Justin could have been there. He was only three at the time, though, and we had decided it was best for him to stay home. Rest assured, he has seen tapes of my Derby victories— many times.

As I left the jockeys' room after showering, I came upon McCarron. While we have not agreed on many issues, he had my respect that day. We had both ridden the races of our lives, with barely a nostril to separate our valiant horses.

I reached out to Chris and offered him two long-stemmed roses.

"Thanks," he said. "I will give them to my daughter. She will love them."

Mr. Young's excitement at the Derby victory he had waited a lifetime for was matched only by his generosity. He sent me a substantial gift a week later as a symbol of his appreciation for the gift I had given him.

As for Grindstone, who had undergone arthroscopic knee surgery as a two-year-old, the immensity of his effort was such that he never raced again.

It did not matter. His reputation for courage was already made.

I THOUGHT A THIRD DERBY HAD MY NAME WRITTEN on it the first time I sat on Empire Maker. Hall of Fame trainer Bobby Frankel asked me to stop by his barn one morning in the fall of 2002, saying there was a horse he wanted me to breeze.

I saw Medaglia d'Oro, a horse I had already enjoyed a great deal of success on, and lifted my leg to climb aboard.

"No," Bobby said. "Work the horse behind him."

I breezed Empire Maker, then a juvenile, in company with three-year-old Medaglia d'Oro for six furlongs. Empire Maker stayed stride for stride with him before yielding grudgingly at the end.

This could be a Triple Crown type of horse, I thought.

That impression grew as Empire Maker won his debut handily to begin a light juvenile campaign. I suggested early in 2003 that the colt, who lacked mental focus, might benefit from blinkers.

Bobby agreed and Empire Maker, with his new headgear, blew them away in the Florida Derby. He toyed with runner-up Funny Cide in the Wood Memorial and went to Churchill Downs as the one to beat. Bobby openly spoke about the chance to win the Triple Crown. No one could blame him.

I still believe that might have been within our grasp if Empire Maker had not bruised his foot during Derby week, forcing him to miss valuable training time. As it was, Bobby, with an eye on the three races, had not pushed him hard before that.

Bobby nonethless assured me the colt would be at his best on Saturday. That belief influenced our decision to choose the twelfth post position when number 5 was still available. Although it meant losing ground, we also believed it increased the chances of a trouble-free trip. Empire Maker would shrug off a few lost lengths on his best day.

I gave the son of Unbridled a wide trip, handling him with supreme confidence. It was misplaced. He was not nearly up to his peak performance and did well to be second. He would skip the Preakness before redeeming himself and denying Funny Cide's Triple Crown bid in the Belmont.

Empire Maker's undoing will always stay with me. It made an emphatic point about margin of error as it concerns the Kentucky Derby.

There is none.

Ten

PERFECT *10*

I love horses. They are magnificent creations, with personali-
ties as entertaining and as complex as human beings. Yet in
dealing with thousands of them over the course of a career, I have
allowed myself to get emotionally attached to only a few. Cigar is
at the top of that very short list.

My introduction to him was far from auspicious, however.
Named for an aviation checkpoint in the Gulf of Mexico by his
owner, Allen Paulson, Cigar was four years old in 1994, and possessed a stunningly ordinary record. The son of a turf horse
named Palace Music, Cigar mostly raced on the turf, and when I
first rode him, he had a 1-for-11 record there as part of an overall
2-for-13 mark.

Yet his trainer, the well-respected Bill Mott, was convinced of his talent. He had tried several different jockeys, searching for someone who could find the key to his enigmatic horse. When he asked me to try, I took a swing at it—and missed just as badly. Cigar handled the grass well enough for me. There was nothing wrong with his stride. There were no breathing issues. He warmed up fine and galloped out well. And yet, at the end of the day, it was another ordinary performance in a string of them. It was another occasion on which he had failed to run to expectations.

Somehow, though, I believed that Bill Mott was right. I analyzed Cigar's past performances like a detective looking for clues. Line after line was scrutinized. Nothing but mediocrity. "There is something more to this horse than meets the eye," I kept telling myself. But I couldn't figure it out. I never wrote him off, but I suspected that he would join a seemingly endless list of Thoroughbreds who appear to have what it takes without ever putting it all together.

Then one night in the fall of 1994, I was competing at the Meadowlands in East Rutherford, New Jersey, when Mike Smith entered the locker room. We had both ridden at Aqueduct earlier that day.

"Did you do any good after I left?" I asked.

"Yes," he replied. "Remember Cigar? He ran off the screen, that's how far he won by."

"On grass?" I asked incredulously.

"No. On dirt."

The next day, I made it my business to arrive at Aqueduct early to watch the replay of Cigar's victory in his switch from turf to dirt. Sure enough, he had won as he pleased by eight lengths. Then I did not think much more about it.

MOTT: *Cigar was bred for turf. He was a nice-looking horse who trained well. It just seemed that when I ran him on turf the first few times, he was much too anxious to be a good turf horse. He was up in the bridle, and he seemed to run himself out of the bit.*

Because he had worked okay on dirt, I thought I would try him on it. I didn't know it would work until I tried it.

Some horses do show talent and they have some class, but they don't get results. You go through the process and use up all avenues: long, short, turf, dirt, different styles of running.

It is always right there in front of you, but sometimes you don't get it right off the bat.

We were standing by the rail watching and wondering what was going to happen. All of a sudden, we saw the real Cigar. He blew his competition away.

I remember Tom Durkin was calling the race and Cigar had set fast fractions. He turned for home and Durkin says, "It's Cigar, and no butts about it!"

Then, approximately three weeks later, my agent, Bob Frieze, called to give me my upcoming mounts. "You are on Cigar in the NYRA Mile," he said, before quickly moving on to the next assignment.

Mott was well known for waiting until the last possible minute to decide on a spot, and in the interim, Mike had committed to trainer H. Allen Jerkens to ride Devil His Due. I had no idea how that turn of events was about to alter my life and career.

Riding Cigar in the NYRA Mile—a race that would later be renamed in his honor—was a revelation to me and to the betting public, which allowed him to go off at odds of nearly 9 to 1.

We were no more than fifty yards out of the gate when I felt an aggressiveness, a surge, that had been missing on turf. He was a totally different horse. He was pulling me along and was ready to tackle the front-runner whenever I gave him his cue.

We were a few lengths off the lead as we approached the final turn. Other jockeys were asking their horses for more, and I was not, yet we were still advancing. I pushed on Cigar slightly—and he roared away from those other horses as if they were standing still. The final margin was seven lengths. It was a stunning turn-around from when I had last ridden him.

Bill had left it to an assistant, Tim Jones, to saddle him and later make sure he cooled out properly, and we both marveled at what had just happened. As befuddling as Cigar had been on turf, he was a machine on dirt.

"Tim," I said, "I think he's the real thing."

That ended the 1994 season for Cigar, but he was very much on my mind when I went to Gulfstream Park for the winter meet. The television replay of his switch to dirt remained vivid. The spirit he'd shown in the NYRA Mile, and the burst he'd given me at the slightest prompting, stuck with me even more.

I would visit the barn from time to time, always with the same question for Bill.

"How is Cigar doing?"

The answer never varied.

"Training well."

Only the summer before, Bill and I had begun to develop a

strong working relationship that would be tremendously benefi-
cial to both of us.

> MOTT: *I remember Jerry and his agent coming up to me one morn-*
> *ing at Saratoga. I was on a pony at the starting gate and Jerry was*
> *not shy at all. "I want to ride some horses for you," he said.*
>
> *He hit me at just about the right time because Mike [Smith] had*
> *bailed out on me on a few horses. I was in a situation where I needed*
> *to find another rider. Jerry wasn't a tough choice.*

Cigar returned from his layoff in a Gulfstream allowance race
on January 2. While he broke a step slow, the second time he hit
the ground, he was in full flight. He was pulling on me every
pole, leaving no doubt as to the outcome.

This was a different horse from the one I had ridden in the
NYRA Mile, however. In that race, he had drawn off when asked.
This time, he established a lead of two to three lengths in the
upper stretch—and that's all he was going to do. He beat Upping
the Ante by a comfortable two lengths.

He would be that way the rest of his life. He was smarter than
I was. It was almost as if he knew we were about to up the ante on
him, that there were massive challenges ahead. He would do
what it took to win, and not expend an ounce of energy more.
He made sure to save something for next time.

My greatest concern with Cigar was not how he finished but
how he started. I always viewed him as a true miler, and yet the
prestigious big-money races were all at a mile and a quarter. If
he was to meet our rapidly growing expectations, he would have
to handle the classic distance. That meant teaching him to be

multidimensional. He would need to relax off the lead and become a stalker rather than a front-runner.

If allowed to, Cigar would have immediately rocketed to the lead. I was able to persuade him to sit off horses. I cannot say I ever got him to relax. Call it a compromise we could both live with.

The season-opening allowance was a prep for a confrontation with Holy Bull in the 1⅛-mile Donn Handicap on February 11. While the event attracted a nine-horse field, I viewed it as a match race between two horses that wanted to burn on the front end. No one else was of their caliber.

Once we drew inside Holy Bull, my task at speed-favoring Gulfstream was clear. There would be no taking Cigar back, not this time. If I had anything to say about it, we would get the jump on Holy Bull and Mike Smith.

In the two races before this, I had been very quiet on Cigar. I had done everything I could to keep him from getting keyed up as we approached the starting gate. This time, just before he stepped in, I tapped him on the right shoulder.

Although that action sounds insignificant, the effect on an aggressive horse like Cigar was profound. Compare it to handing a compulsive gambler a fistful of one-hundred-dollar bills. He was ready to spring into action.

The race was on from the first jump. I had thrown down the gauntlet. Mike was going to have to use Holy Bull awfully hard and ask him to run unmercifully fast if he was to make the lead. We fairly flew into the first turn.

This is a blast! I thought. *This is what racing is all about.*

I knew Holy Bull was great. He had already proved that to me when he beat me on Concern in the Travers. As Holy Bull exerted pressure with every stride, I was about to find out how good Cigar was.

Just about the time we hit the backside, there was a loud pop amid the pounding of hooves. Mike cursed. Suddenly, Holy Bull was nowhere to be seen.

I knew what had happened.

No time for sympathy or sorrow. Time to change plans. If Holy Bull had broken down under the strain of the pace, what toll might it take on Cigar?

While it was imperative that I slow him down, only so much could be done. I had given him the signal to go, go, go. He had taken it. He wasn't giving it back.

Too late to change your mind, jock.

Given the ease with which Cigar was traveling, I started to think, *Maybe he can keep this up.* To my delight, he did, coasting by five and a half lengths.

But the result was bittersweet at best. As much as I had wanted to defeat Holy Bull, there was no satisfaction in winning this way. Holy Bull had ruptured a tendon in his left foreleg. While the injury was not life-threatening, he would never flash his speed again. Racing had lost yet another star.

I felt sorry for the connections, and especially for Mike. It is hard enough to get a good horse. There is no consolation when you lose one.

This may sound cold, but I have no choice except to treat horses the way a doctor views his patients. You try not to get too close—because inevitably you will lose some. Cigar was one of the very few exceptions.

Next was the $500,000 Gulfstream Park Handicap, and I viewed it as a major test, not because of the competition, which came up soft, but simply because it was run at a mile and a quarter. Would Cigar go that far? Would he rate?

Cigar was so smart. It was almost as if he knew what needed to be done just as well as I did. I never moved on him and he galloped out powerfully after being the best by seven and a half lengths. He could go the distance, all right.

I had not felt this kind of excitement since the first time I'd been struck by Derby Fever. I was at Bill's barn every day. Cigar was so neat to be around. I could take little Justin up to him thirty minutes after a race and allow him to pat him on the nose. The show of affection was gratefully accepted.

SUZEE: *It was wonderful to see someone who never wanted a dog in the house, who was so reserved, beginning to allow himself some emotions. He loved Cigar, and I was so happy to see him enjoy every moment that horse brought to us.*

Before a race? I kept my son as far away as possible. Cigar was clever enough to know that a race was approaching, because his training became increasingly serious and his workouts were more strenuous. I swear it, he would put his game face on.

I once stroked his neck a couple of days before a race. He shook his head as if to scold me. "Look, this is not playtime. This is work, and I have no time for this nonsense."

Cigar's next stop was the $750,000 Oaklawn Park Handicap. Rather than head to Arkansas, Suzee and Justin accompanied me on my annual migration to Lexington, Kentucky, for the spring meet at Keeneland.

Among my mounts there was a two-year-old named Gregory

Hines. He was a first-time starter, and that alone makes jockeys wary.

While I was on alert, however, there was nothing I could do when Gregory Hines, startled by something in the crowd, ducked out into the pony, causing me to fall off. I landed on my feet, even with the saddle, and had the presence of mind to keep the right rein in my hand. I did not want him to run off and perhaps do irreparable harm to himself or someone else.

That did not prevent my frightened mount from damaging me. He wheeled and kicked me in the chest. I felt as though a cannonball had blown through me. I went down immediately, gasping for air.

Even as I struggled for every breath, I thought of Cigar. Even as they loaded me into the ambulance, I wondered if I could recover in time for his next start, three days away.

Such is the life of a jockey. Such is the anxiety he feels when faced with the possibility of missing a big race with a big horse. It also is the nature of the business that at least ten agents speed-dialed Bill to let him know their rider was ready as a replacement. Just doing their jobs.

Once I arrived at the hospital, X-rays showed I had a severely bruised sternum and bruised ribs. Since I am an alcoholic, I declined a prescription for a heavy-duty painkiller. I could not chance any substance that might eventually lead to dependence.

SUZEE: *I remember Jerry sitting in the emergency room looking so hurt, not just physically but emotionally. I knew he was worrying about Cigar and whether he would make his next race. I was grateful his flak jacket had kept him from a more severe injury and that Justin was too young to understand the pain his father was enduring.*

I called Bill, who said he would arrange for a backup if I could not make it. I would not attempt to ride Cigar if I could not give him my best.

Although I have a high threshhold for pain, willpower was no match for the agony I experienced when I returned to the house we had rented for the meet. I writhed in pain on the bathroom floor. My breathing was extremely shallow. I could not take a full breath.

I had to think of something—and fast.

Suzee filled Ziploc bags with ice and placed a layer of them under my back and on top of my chest. I was a Popsicle. After ten minutes or so, my body went numb. Exhausted from the stress of the day, I somehow managed to fall asleep.

It was a drastic measure, all right. It also was my only chance to make it back in time. By noon the next day, I felt dramatically better. I still took the afternoon off but was able to return on Friday, albeit at a bit less than 100 percent. I could not look Billy in the eye and reassure him I could do the job on Saturday if I was still unable to do it on Friday.

I made it through the day at Keeneland and then headed to Arkansas. As I arrived at the paddock for the Oaklawn Park Handicap, however, my health was only one of my worries. The field was stacked with legitimate contenders, starting with Concern, whom I had ridden to victory in the 1994 Breeders' Cup Classic.

For every mount, there is a story. Concern was no different. I had flown to New Orleans to work him for his initial start in 1995. You would think a jockey would have a slight margin for error after producing a Breeders' Cup victory. Not so with Dickie Small, Concern's trainer.

There are two finish wires at the Fair Grounds. In working Concern between races, I mistakenly took him to the wrong wire. Small was upset, to say the least.

"You're off the horse," he barked into the phone.

I asked for an explanation.

"You misjudged the work, and you don't even know who my exercise riders are."

"Dickie, you're right," I said. "I'm from out of town, so I don't know your exercise riders personally. But I know their names from the checks I wrote to thank them for their part in the Breeders' Cup."

I know at least one agent had been telling Dickie I was going to choose Cigar whenever both were targeted for the same spot. He made sure to beat me to the punch before a conflict arose. Not the classiest move.

Anyway, I knew Concern could be as feisty as his trainer. There also was multimillionaire Best Pal, Santa Anita Handicap champ Urgent Request and Silver Goblin, who was sure to look for his ninth consecutive victory by gunning for the lead.

Cigar was pulling during the post parade, so I knew I had plenty of horse beneath me. He could be so docile around the barn. Put a tack and a rider on his back, however, and it was as if he transformed into a racing machine.

He was full of life just walking around the shedrow, and he possessed a huge stride. I once timed him. He completed the loop 15 seconds faster than any other horse in the barn.

The tug I felt throughout the post parade filled me with confidence. I kept Cigar four to five lengths off the early lead set, as expected, by Silver Goblin. He started picking off horses on his own as we approached the far turn. We were bearing down on the leader.

I always tried to maneuver Cigar close to his chief rivals because I believed he beat them well before the wire through intimidation. Just as boxers stand toe-to-toe, nose-to-nose before a bout, waiting for the other to blink, this was no different.

As Cigar reached Silver Goblin's flank and we prepared to stare him down, his jockey, Dale Cordova, sensed the urgency of the moment. He reached high to whip his horse and inadvertently struck Cigar in the face.

That will discourage most horses, and they will begin to back up. Not my guy. He flinched, then threw it into another gear I had never felt before. We blew past Silver Goblin, who was still striding out, in the blink of an eye.

Cordova later apologized. No need. He had accidentally contributed to our win, by two and a half lengths.

That kind of response enhances a horse's reputation, so it was hardly surprising when the competition for the next race, the $600,000 Pimlico Special, came up thin. Concern was taking another crack at us. Devil His Due was there as well. Nothing but suspects followed them.

One thought recurred to me: Cigar represented the only early foot; Pimlico is annually a speed-favoring track. I would take advantage of that by granting Cigar's wish this time and allowing him to set a deliberate pace. That's exactly the way it happened. The result: An easy two-and-a-quarter-length margin against Devil His Due.

Although it was Triple Crown season, my mind was always on Cigar. I was at the barn seven days a week now, watching him follow his morning routine. He would go to the track every day at approximately 7 A.M., whether it was to gallop or for a work. He would return for his morning bath. Shortly before 8 A.M., Erma Scott, his hot walker, would graze him in an enclosed area behind the Mott barn at Belmont Park.

I liked to sit on a fencepost and watch Cigar feast on the lush grass. There was something wonderfully peaceful about that time. This horse had more of a presence to him than many people I know. I am quite sure he knew he was special. And I am certain he craved attention. Cameras did not bother him at all. In fact, he was a bit of a ham as he paraded in front of film crews who regularly called on him.

Cigar seemed to know everyone around the barn and what that person might do for him. When he was done grazing, he would walk over to me as I sat on the fence. He would put his face about two inches from mine as if to say, "I can push you over anytime I please."

When he was a foal, those who worked around him nicknamed him "The Hammer." Throughout his career, he was very much in charge. And he made sure everyone knew it.

Cigar received all of the adulation he wanted before the June 3 Massachusetts Handicap, thanks to the good people at Suffolk Downs. They arranged for a police escort to meet his van at the Massachusetts border. "Welcome Cigar!" read billboard after billboard as we made our way to the track.

By this point in my career, I had been thrilled to win the Kentucky Derby, the Preakness, the Belmont Stakes and the Breeders' Cup Classic. All of those days were monumental. Nothing, however, approached the excitement that surrounded this horse.

This was not about money for the fans. No one was getting

rich by betting Cigar. His four-and-a-half-length walk in the park against aptly named runner-up Poor But Honest in the Mass Cap returned but twenty cents on the dollar. No, this was about a glimpse at greatness.

Bill was very much the son of Dr. Tom Mott, who was known as "The Flying Veterinarian." From the time Bill trained his first winner at age fifteen, the South Dakota native built a reputation for protecting his horses. He's the only trainer I know who, if he won the Kentucky Derby, would truly debate whether it was in the horse's interest to go on to the Preakness, the second leg of the Triple Crown.

Bill was eager to give Cigar a break after he returned to Belmont Park from Massachusetts, but Allen Paulson was much more of a roll-the-dice guy, and he had other thoughts. The son of an Iowa farmer, Mr. Paulson embodied the American Dream. His red, white and blue silks, which would grace seven champions and more than a hundred stakes winners, reflected his patriotism. He believed in hard work and pushed himself harder than anyone while building Gulfstream Aerospace Technologies into a powerful company. "I've never met a lucky lazy guy," he would always say.

All of his decisions were based on risk versus reward. He did not fear taking chances. In June 1987, he had flown his Gulfstream IV around the world in record time. He set twenty-four world speed records by the time he was done.

Risk versus reward. That formula, and Allen's very makeup, were telling him not to stop on Cigar. He wanted to press on.

As an added incentive, Hollywood Park bumped the purse of the July 2 Hollywood Gold Cup from $750,000 to one million in reaching out to a former member of its board of directors. As if all of that was not enough, Allen lived on the West Coast. Who could blame him for wanting to show off his prized possession in his backyard?

Bill understood. Even if he hadn't, Allen was in charge. As conservative as Bill was, he admitted the boss was right.

Results did not hint at a dropoff. Cigar was training with his usual vigor. He was attacking the feed tub. Most horses would have needed a break right around this time. Cigar was not most horses.

He handled the coast-to-coast trek with ease. He clip-clopped off that plane with his chest out as if he were the president visiting foreign dignitaries.

I did not always enjoy the West Coast trip because there were a few riders there who were more concerned with trying to beat a specific horse than with trying to win themselves. These knuckleheads are happy to play the spoiler role, even if it comes at the expense of the owner and trainer they are working for.

It was not unexpected, but still a concern, when Cigar was forced well out around the first turn in the Gold Cup. It was always my goal to make his races as easy and as incident-free as possible.

My eyes were always on the prize—the $3 million Breeders' Cup Classic, to be run at his home track, Belmont Park, at the end of October. If we could get him there in form, without bumps and bruises, he was money in the bank.

There was nothing any other rider could do to stop Cigar at Hollywood Park. Losing a couple of lengths meant nothing to him. He was four wide at one point; neither of us would allow that to go on for very long. He made an early lead, and one of the strongest races of his career led to a commanding three-and-a-half-length margin against Tinners Way at the end of the 1¼ miles.

Seven starts in 1995, seven victories.

Mr. Paulson was so happy and so proud. It was the moment owners live for—a decisive victory in front of family and friends by a horse he had bred.

"Did he feel as good as he looked?" he asked breathlessly.

Indeed, he had.

The joy of Allen and his wife, Madeleine, was matched only by mine and Bill's. I delighted in knowing that the same fans who hooted and hollered when Cigar was saddled were now shouting and cheering for a horse they recognized as the best on either coast. A skeptical West Coast media, many of whom did not expect him to crack the top three, had also been converted.

Bill was as much relieved as he was happy. He had wanted to back off the horse. Mr. Paulson would now grant that wish. Cigar was given more than two months away from the races. He was stabled at Saratoga Race Course, which allowed him to breathe deeply of the country air and enjoy the warm summer nights— and then it was back to work.

Bill planned two Belmont Park preps leading to the Classic: the 1⅛-mile Woodward on September 16, and the 1¼-mile Jockey Club Gold Cup on October 7.

In the Woodward, Cigar toyed with a six-horse field, topping Star Standard by two and three-quarter lengths. The comment line in the past performances was an exact description: "Under wraps."

Eight for eight!

The Jockey Club Gold Cup was a seven-wide adventure. Still, I never doubted the outcome. Once we made the lead by the top of the stretch, there was no overtaking Cigar. He finished a length better than Unaccounted For.

Nine for nine!

One race to go—and many hurdles to overcome in the Breeders' Cup Classic—to complete a perfect season.

I'm the kind of guy who wants everything to go according to plan, starting with my walk from the jockeys' room to the paddock. Suddenly, all of the vibes were bad.

Seven days before the big event, Cigar apparently ate something that disagreed with him and broke out in hives. Once that condition cleared up and we could focus on the race, the distance was a major concern. Although Cigar had certainly shown an ability to handle a mile and a quarter, he was much better suited to a furlong or two shorter. It did not help, either, that he drew far outside, post 10, in a field of the eleven best horses the racing world could muster.

Then the weather became a huge headache. We spent the days leading to the Classic with one eye on the horse and another on the sky, where angry storm clouds seemed to be forever gathering. He had neither trained nor raced in the mud, so that condition represented a great unknown. And this meticulous planner detested the unknown.

BILL MOTT: *The barn flooded the night before the Classic. We were in there bailing out the water until 7 A.M. on race day. I finally took Cigar to the track. I wasn't feeling too good about anything. I had thought about scratching him, but only briefly. It's not like you can go out and find another $3 million race.*

For whatever reason, he seemed so sharp when he got to the main track to stretch his legs. He was bucking and squealing. I said to myself, "I think this sucker will handle it."

Bill conveyed to me how well the morning had gone once the flooded shedrow was cleared. Still, we both would have been more at ease with a fast surface instead of a track that had been sealed. The dirt is packed tightly during that process, forcing water to run off rather than seep in. Despite a Herculean effort by the track superintendent and his crew, we would run in the mud.

Upon reaching the paddock, there was yet another unwelcome issue. Bobby Frankel, the trainer of Tinners Way, believed Cigar had been improperly shod to give him better traction. He requested that the shoes be inspected, and the paddock blacksmith was obligated to do so.

This forced Cigar to remain in the saddling area longer than usual. As he watched his rivals leave for the track while he was made to lift one leg after another, he was not at all happy. His muscles tightened. He began prancing and kicking and generally carrying on.

Bill wasn't happy, either. They were the same shoes Cigar had worn all season. If Frankel was going to pull the upset, he thought there was a better way to go about it. Needless to say, the shoes were approved.

I could finally turn my thoughts to the race. Unaccounted For, Tinners Way, Concern and Soul of the Matter were among the hard-hitting older horses. French Deputy and Peaks and Valleys were dangerous three-year-olds. Halling, brought over from Europe, was a curious entry. The four-year-old had spun off eight consecutive victories, but on grass.

Cigar warmed up well, giving me confidence he would handle the mud as well as he had dealt with everything else since his long and arduous campaign began in January. I knew the start, and our ability to overcome that outside post, would be critical to the outcome. For the sake of positioning, he needed to give me an early burst. The explosion would have to come later.

Sure enough, the early spark was there. Predictably, Star Standard spurted to the lead during the short run into the first turn. L'Carriere prompted him in second. I eased Cigar back to third, never worse than a length or two behind.

Cigar was eager. I was patient. Cigar was pulling, straining to be set free. I kept my tight hold, knowing it would be disastrous if I gave him the nod too soon. The tug-of-war, waged through the opening six furlongs, was plain to see as far away as the announcer's stand.

"Cigar wants to go," Tom Durkin roared, "but Jerry Bailey says, 'No, not yet!'"

We reached the far turn . . . and there was no restraining him any longer. He was three wide, only a length and a half from the front, and he was screaming for the lead. My weary arms were telling me to let him have it.

Unaccounted For and Pat Day were starting to unleash their move inside.

Time to go.

I opened my fingers ever so slightly. Nothing could have prepared me for the forcefulness of his move.

"Three furlongs to go," said Durkin, his voice rising to meet the moment. "Cigar! Cigar makes his move and he sweeps to the lead with a dramatic rush as Jerry Bailey turns him loose!"

We stormed to the lead by the quarter pole. Unaccounted For was out of answers. But Jorge Chavez was in a furious drive with L'Carriere.

Time to go.

I switched the stick from left to right. Whack!

Cigar was gone.

Durkin captured the magnificence of the stretch run with a sentence that was one long exclamation point.

"And here he is," Durkin cried, "the unconquerable, invincible, unbeatable Cigar!"

The margin was a typical two and a half lengths against runner-up L'Carriere, who was not going to cut into that no matter how many more times we had gone around.

Ten-for-ten! An undefeated season!

After years of striving for perfection, only to realize how imperfect I was, Cigar, with a tour de force that required only 1:59⅖ seconds, finally showed me what unstained excellence is like.

MOTT: *There are always so many guesses and hunches in horse racing, so many different factors come into play and it's so competitive. You never have the same situation twice. Never.*

When he won, it culminated such a wonderful year and a wonderful run. When I congratulated Jerry, there wasn't much that had to be said. We got it done. I think we both knew we were on a very special mission. We both realized it was a very special time.

I remember how Jerry used to come to the barn and just sit and watch him. We were both experienced enough to know we were seeing something extraordinary.

I was loving the moment. I arrived at the postrace news conference with a cigar clenched between my teeth. Racing's long-awaited superstar had earned $4,819,800 during an odyssey that had taken us from one coast to another, to six tracks in six states.

His overall winning streak stood at twelve, four short of the record set by the mighty Citation from 1948 to 1950. Naturally, there were questions about what 1996 might hold for the two of us.

After missing an Eclipse as the nation's outstanding jockey in other years I felt I was deserving, I would not be denied this time, and I was right. As for Cigar, he was about to be named Horse of the Year, a title that did not begin to describe his domination.

"I don't know if he can duplicate this year," I told members of the media. "I don't know if that's possible for him or anybody else."

When I embraced Suzee and Justin afterward, we knew we were having the ride of our lives. And it was not nearly over.

Eleven

DANCING IN THE DESERT

*R*isk versus reward.

Sheikh Mohammed bin Rashid Al Maktoum, the Crown Prince of Dubai, spent considerable time and effort to recruit Cigar for the inaugural running of the Dubai World Cup. My suspicion, though, is that neither he nor his advisers needed to say a word to draw Allen Paulson's interest.

When Allen evaluated the proposition on his usual terms—risk versus reward—he saw the trip as a slam dunk. Since the summer of 1995, when he first heard about Sheikh Mohammed's brainstorm to host a race that would draw attention to his remote homeland while attracting the finest horses in the world, Allen was interested.

He relished all kinds of challenges. Since he viewed Cigar as practically indestructible as well as unbeatable, he saw minimal risk. As for the reward, well, there were four million reasons to go.

"I think Cigar can do that," Allen said at first mention of the $4 million World Cup.

Of course, Allen believed Cigar could do most anything.

Bill and I were game to go to Dubai, but we knew what a daunting proposition it would be. This was not a matter of shipping from the East Coast to the West Coast, a trip known to sap many a horse. This was a journey halfway around the world to compete on a surface that would be unlike anything Cigar had ever experienced. He would face the best at the classic distance of a mile and a quarter, which was not his best.

Even if the horse withstood this, what would he have left for the rest of the year after his March 27 date with international fame and potential fortune?

For racing, that first World Cup was like man walking on the moon. We had seen pictures of the surface but had little idea of its composition or how Cigar would react when he sank his hoof into it. This was no small step for a horse, and we would have to travel farther than anyone else to take it.

At the same time, we all possessed the confidence that we would be going with the best horse in the world—assuming he was at the top of his game. The first issue was elevating him to that peak.

Bill planned to use a combination of stiff workouts and two solid races, the Donn Handicap in Florida and the March 2 Santa Anita Handicap at Santa Anita Park, to achieve that.

Cigar jousted briefly with Wekiva Springs before handling the February 10 Donn with two-length ease. But a problem surfaced not long after that race. He was found to have a bruised right front foot.

Since noted blacksmith Jim Bayes could not immediately fly out of Arkansas due to fog, Bill reverted to the training his father had given him and removed the shoe. He scraped the hoof, then cut away and drained the abscessed area. Finally, a patch was applied to protect the injured portion of the hoof.

Cigar missed thirteen days of training. With that, it became impossible to make the Santa Anita Handicap, a much-needed prep race. Bill was left with no choice but to squeeze three works into an eight-day period before Cigar embarked for Dubai and the great unknown.

Bill was not going to put him through this unless he was convinced Cigar was in condition to win. The decision about whether the horse was fit enough went down to the last day and to how the horse performed in a seven-furlong test.

"If I get a good seven-furlong work into him," Bill said, "we'll go."

Cigar wasn't usually a sharp worker. He knew when it was time to prove himself—and it wasn't the morning. In an effort to spur him, he worked the seven furlongs in company. Boy, did he put on a show! He tore through the drill in 1:23 at Gulfstream.

Now we could be sure we were sending Cigar, not some impostor.

He was given intravenous fluids before a ship that had never before been attempted. We watched with an unsettling mix of hope and dread as the horse who meant so much to us, so much to the world, walked proudly into the van that would take him to the airport.

He was accompanied, of course, by Snowball, the gentle white pony who was his companion. Rest assured, Snowball was accorded the same first-class treatment, for he was as much a part of the team as anyone.

Bill was next to take flight. The first time I called him in Dubai to check on Cigar, I wondered if I would be able to hear him. His voice came across as clearly as if we were standing beside each other.

I wanted to make sure I did what little I could do to prepare. Suzee and I set out five days before the race, taking an overnight flight from Miami to London during which we both slept, then boarding Air Emirates for the second and much longer leg. We were on the move for approximately twenty-four hours from initial takeoff to a destination so different that it seemed worlds away.

We were struck immediately by the high temperatures and the equally high level of security. Remember, the horror that was 9/11 was years away, so the sight of guards bearing machine guns at the airport was unsettling as we retrieved our luggage and golf clubs.

Sheikh Mohammed had sent his representatives to whisk us through customs. They were attentive to our group throughout our stay. They even granted an immigration waiver to allow Madeleine Paulson to be accompanied by Oliver, her beloved Jack Russell terrier.

When we arrived at the hotel, Suzee and I stood on our balcony and admired the Persian Gulf. I could not help but think back to my first trip away from my parents' home and how that hot, old bus had labored to transport us from El Paso to Denver. How far the sport had taken me since then!

Then my thoughts immediately shifted to the race. Cigar had

been off his feed since he landed. Even Snowball, always raven-
ous, had failed to lick his tub clean.

We hoped that a half-mile work, scheduled shortly after I
arrived, would help put Cigar back on his toes. We went to the
track in the evening. It was much cooler then, and the World Cup
would be held at night.

Bill accompanied us to the track on Snowball. We both were
heartened by the sight of Cigar pulling off the pony. He was feeling himself again and was ready to strut his stuff. He was not content with the half-mile drill that was intended. He would not let
up until he had gone five-eighths and there wasn't a darn thing I
could do about it.

Not that I was at all displeased. This was Cigar's way of telling
us he was in tip-top shape. He had overcome the travel, he was
handling the heavy, sandy racecourse, and now it was up to the
two of us to deal with the competition.

At this point, I was more concerned about my ability to meet
the challenge than I was Cigar's. A great part of my success
depended on knowing my competition and anticipating the
action. In this case, I could not obtain past performances for
many of the horses. Just as meticulous preparation always filled
me with confidence, lack of preparation made me uneasy.

Then there was the layout and makeup of Nad Al Sheba, so
different from anything we had ever been on. Its yawning
stretch, more than three furlongs in length, was of particular
concern. Cigar was accustomed to my allowing him to run free
through the stretch. Could I persuade him to hold back a bit
longer without engaging in a wrestling match that would exhaust
us both?

Everything was new and different to Cigar, too. Frankly, he

was dealing with it a lot better than me. Here I was trying to prepare for the unexpected. Good luck.

Nad Al Sheba does not typically allow ponies to accompany horses onto the track. I told Bill it was imperative that Cigar have Snowball at his side. Otherwise, I was afraid he would run off with me, and the race would be over before it ever started. The racing authorities understood my predicament and waived the rule.

That night, the World Cup Gala, a dinner-dance held at a first-class hotel on the beach, provided a romantic evening with Suzee and a respite from my cares. Sheikh Mohammed had arranged for Simply Red, a British band, to provide entertainment. The food was the best international fare imaginable. If any of us ever envisioned Dubai as a backward part of the world, we knew better now.

SUZEE: *It was a magical evening. I remember that we were dancing beneath the stars, holding each other close, as the band played, "If You Don't Know Me By Now." After all we had been through, it felt so good to be in the arms of my husband in this fairy-tale setting that was wonderfully real. I felt as though all of the foreign riders were checking out the big-name rider from America, wondering what he was made of.*

I was as excited as could be when race day came. The card was to begin at 5 P.M. I walked the course three hours before that. It was not at all like what it had been in previous days. They had transformed it into an extremely fast surface, much faster and deeper than the one we had worked over.

As you know by now, I don't like surprises. Here was one I could do nothing about. After that, I sat in the jocks' room for what felt like an eternity, waiting for the World Cup. Usually, my time is spent studying the *Daily Racing Form,* calculating where every horse would be at certain junctures. I never stray from this routine, whether the race involves claiming horses or million-dollar babies.

I had gone to school on our rivals from the United States—Soul of the Matter, owned by singer and songwriter Burt Bacharach, and L'Carriere. But then there was Pentire, the pride of Great Britain; Lively Mount, who represented Japan; Danewin, the best Australia could put forward; and four horses who enjoyed a significant advantage simply because they were based in Dubai.

As I pondered how the World Cup might unfold, I knew exactly what Olympic athletes feel like. Allen's red, white and blue silks never felt so right. The opportunity to represent my country well meant as much to me as the very big purse.

When Cigar entered the saddling area, he looked every bit the champion that he was. He had put his jet lag behind him and was feeling as bright as he looked.

It was almost sunset as race time neared. Hundreds of Sudanese Muslims, dressed in white, prostrated themselves in prayer. For a minute, it appeared they were worshipping Cigar.

Bill's pre-race instructions were the same as they had been in New York, Florida or California. "Get him out of there and keep him moving. Good luck." His game plan for me was more detailed with other horses. Nothing more needed to be said when it came to Cigar.

I knew this horse the way a father knows his son or daughter. I knew what made him tick and what ticked him off. I knew that there would be a time in every race when we would reverse roles and he would be the captain while I would be the passenger, hanging on and hoping for another on-time arrival.

In the World Cup, I would have to plead with Cigar not to assert himself too soon. Otherwise, that long stretch would be sure to dash our hopes and dreams.

Cigar, breaking from post 10 in a field of eleven, was off slowly. His right hind foot did not initially grip the deep sand, and by the time he recovered, we were no better than mid-pack, with L'Carriere having hustled to a lead that was soon pressured by Danewin and Lively Mount. Soul of the Matter, and Gary Stevens, were nowhere to be found in the tangle of horses around me.

I was delighted to see the heat being put on L'Carriere. I felt sure he would wilt. I was less than pleased, however, with what Cigar was giving me. Or not giving me. He was only a few jumps from the lead, but not pulling me along with his usual vigor.

I waited.

I asked him slightly to make sure he would hold his position, and he responded. Otherwise, I had no choice but to go with the flow. Any sign of distress on my part would rouse him early, and then it was certain he could not sustain that extended run to the wire.

I waited.

We turned for home just half a length off the lead. That was the good news. The very bad news was that Cigar was still not tugging, still not ready to take command.

I waited.

Then I saw a shadow, insignificant at first but growing larger and more menacing all the time. I glanced back. Soul of the Matter, having been reserved by Stevens for one hellacious run, was attacking.

I could wait no longer.

I shook up the reins, the surest sign I could give to Cigar that it was time to go, go, go. He was like a car with a low battery on a wintry Midwest night. A couple of clicks, then nothing.

There had to be something. With Soul of the Matter bearing down on us, it was up to me to find it.

I lashed Cigar once on his right side. Soul of the Matter had drawn even, then appeared to stick his nose in front. But my horse's enormous engine had finally started.

Cigar had always run well from a left-handed stick. I had been reluctant to switch to that side because they required us to use a shorter whip and I had concerns about dropping it.

There was no choice now—and no room for a fumble.

The stick was in my left hand in a flash. Skeptics had always questioned how Cigar would react when confronted by a chal-lenger who absolutely refused to blink. We were about to find out.

As we rapidly approached the wire, an inseparable pair, Cigar fought as if survival itself was at stake.

I cracked Cigar left-handed. He surged in front by a head.

Another crack. Another hard-fought gain. We flashed across the finish line half a length ahead in 2:03⅖ seconds. It was a scorching duel that had no loser.

"I've never been more proud of a horse finishing second," trainer Richard Mandella rightly said of Soul of the Matter.

"I thought I had you, man," Gary shouted as he extended his hand to me.

Bill, whose training brilliance had allowed Cigar to overcome so many obstacles, was ecstatic as he greeted us. Then he spoke to reporters.

"Our job is to prove the horse is as good as we think he is," he told them. "Conditions might not have been ideal. But then life isn't always ideal. He had to reach down and find a little more today than he ever has before."

Sheikh Mohammed was as overjoyed as anyone as he presented me with a gold whip as a trophy, describing our triumph as a "dream result." He knew the World Cup would have been doomed to a short life if Cigar had not shown that a horse can travel from the United States, cope with the demands of the previously untried event and prevail. Now, the World Cup was validated.

After watching a Dubai woman scramble to retrieve some of Cigar's droppings, Allen expressed the hope that fans back home could grasp the magnitude of what had been accomplished.

"It is a shame that sometimes the great horses, the great in anything, must first die before they are truly appreciated. Cigar has won fourteen straight races. He has traveled halfway around the world. He has done so much," Allen said. "I just hope everyone recognizes just what a special animal he is."

It was a magical experience for me to know we had succeeded at something that had never been attempted before. As important as it had been for me to bring home the roses in the Kentucky Derby, this was every bit as meaningful. It was part of my growing résumé that no one could ever take away.

I had never been so proud of Cigar and also never so proud to be an American. Perhaps I had to venture that far away from the United States to truly appreciate it.

My family and I live well, with magnificent homes in Florida and Saratoga Springs, New York. I never take it for granted and am always grateful to be living in what is truly the "Land of Opportunity." I have no doubt that if a person works hard, he can accomplish whatever he wants and I'm the living proof. I wasn't exactly connected when I started in racing. No agent would even take me when I started. Yet I went on to earn millions of dollars and achieve financial security.

Those thoughts made the flight home less arduous. When we landed, though, I suddenly had a very big care in the world. Bill had brought Cigar out of his stall into the hot morning sun and found that he was almost too drained to walk. He just wanted to stand. He showed no interest in food. While he had won his brawl with Soul of the Matter, no one could have guessed it from his battered appearance.

His $2.4 million share of the purse had allowed him to surpass Alysheba as North America's leading money winner with $7,669,015 in earnings. His fourteen consecutive victories equaled Man o' War's streak and moved him to within two wins of the North American record pounded out by Citation from 1948 to 1950.

There was more to do. But the morning after the World Cup, we wondered if we had already asked more than flesh and bones could bear.

Twelve

MATCHING GREATNESS

*C*igar returned to New York and Bill gave him all the time he needed to recuperate. No one knew how long that would be because no horse had ever been asked to do so much so far from home.

In a matter of weeks, we were all grateful to see the six-year-old gradually return to being the horse we knew and so loved. He was soon eating voraciously again, regaining the pounds he had lost during his ordeal. His head no longer drooped. His countenance was bright.

Once he was back on the track, Bill asked for a little more and a little more each morning. Each time, Cigar gave like a generous parishioner. A race came into focus in our bid for a fifteenth consecutive victory—the $500,000 Massachusetts Handicap.

Everything about that spot made sense. We had won the same event at Suffolk Downs the year before, so we were confident in the track itself. The 1⅛-mile distance would hit our horse between the eyes. Then, last and certainly not least, we had not forgotten how warmly we had been received there.

Sure enough, the race was heavily promoted with a clever television advertisement that ended, "If you miss the Mass Cap, stick around. You might see another horse this great in fifty years or so." Fans saluted Cigar with T-shirts that read "The Second Coming!" Their cheers followed us to the starting gate.

Although the competition was light, our weight assignment was a hefty 130 pounds. That worried me. Even more, I had no idea what I would have under me that June 1, a little more than two months after our previous race was run halfway around the world.

My fears were allayed after a hundred yards. Cigar was ready to go whenever I asked. His long, powerful stride was so reassuring. *He's a phenomenal horse,* I thought to myself, *and he's back.*

Once that stress was gone, there was no strain. I allowed Cigar to take early control and he was a very comfortable two-and-a-quarter-length victor against Personal Merit in a small field of six.

Talk immediately shifted to where we would take our shot at history and the opportunity to match Citation's sixteen-race winning streak. He had started his North American–record run on April 17, 1948, in a stretch that included the Triple Crown, and not stopped until January 26, 1950.

Many tracks reached out, wanting to be part of what would be an unforgettable day, win or lose. They courted Allen in every way possible, including purse supplements.

We expected New York to make its push since that was Cigar's home base. Guess we expected too much. The New York Racing Association made it abundantly clear it would not alter its stakes program for any horse, even one widely viewed as the Horse of the World.

We regretted that NYRA missed an opportunity, but Allen did what he had to do. He never forgot the bottom line in what was an important business decision. It should not surprise anyone that money talked and the rest walked.

Richard Duchossois, the enthusiastic owner of Arlington Park near Chicago, conceived of the Citation Challenge. The special event would carry a purse of $1,075,000 and be run on July 13 at the accommodating distance of 1⅛ miles. As if that was not enough, the race represented a sentimental journey for Allen, whose roots were in Clinton, Iowa.

We were there.

So were 34,223 boisterous fans. As I had handicapped the race, there were two main threats, Dramatic Gold and Unbridled's Song. Other than that, all manes and tails.

I was looking for some early life from Cigar since we broke from the far outside in post 10. It wasn't there, costing us significant ground around the first turn. Honour and Glory carved out the early fractions, while Mike Smith shadowed Cigar with Unbridled's Song.

We were within a couple of lengths of the lead midway through the backstretch, which was fine. As we headed for home, Corey Nakatani and Dramatic Gold forced us far from the rail. If there was a margin for error, it had vanished when we were carried five wide around each turn.

Time to ask Cigar, and not gently.

When he was in form, his reaction to my prompt was instantaneous and his move was a sight to behold, almost as if the rest were running in place.

This was a slow acceleration, like a long freight train lurching under way, as he built momentum needed to overtake Dramatic Gold. I pumped his neck and did not relax until we hit the wire. In the end, Cigar's class and courage made him much the best, by three and half lengths.

Sixteen in a row! A share of the North American record! Our place in immortality beside Citation!

The ovation from fans who had filled Arlington Park all the way up to the cheap seats lasted nearly twenty minutes. While they had not seen Cigar at his best, that made the Citation Challenge even more impressive.

The great ones find a way.

They hailed him as a conquering hero when he returned to the grandstand. They roared when he entered the winner's circle, a bounce still to his step, and primped for the cameras. There was another hurrah when I dismounted, and yet another as he was led away, having done all that could be asked and more for an astounding sixteenth consecutive time.

SUZEE: *Since I'm from Illinois, I must have had thirty family members at the race. The winner's circle can be a very private moment. But the Paulsons were so gracious by allowing my family to be part of it, and they did it with smiles on their faces.*

Cigar had defeated twenty-eight Grade 1 winners at distances ranging from a mile to a mile and a quarter at nine racetracks. He had earned $8,819,815 during that mind-boggling stretch. The numbers were numbing. Still, we were insatiable.

We wanted Cigar to stand alone in history. We wanted number seventeen—and we wanted it badly.

If it was to happen, Allen yearned for it to be on the West Coast. The 1¼-mile Pacific Classic, on August 10 at Del Mar, was circled on the calendar.

Cigar was shipped from Chicago to Saratoga Springs, with its excellent training track and cool country nights. He loved it there, and fans in upstate New York loved him. More than five thousand people clustered at trackside when he worked there for the final time before shipping west. They did not mind the early hour of the drill, 6:45 A.M. They would have stayed awake all night, if necessary, for a glimpse of the horse with a chance to do what no North American Thoroughbred had ever done.

Although Cigar trained well, that last race deeply concerned me. I had described to Bill the slow response, the lack of zip at first asking. Were those telltale signs of a horse who was souring?

Bill was asking that same question. Yet there was nothing in the horse's actions that said we should not press on to the Pacific Classic. He had handled coast-to-coast travel well the year before, a fact not lost on Allen.

Cigar had concerned us before—and always delivered.

The odds for success seemed to improve when trainer Richard Mandella was forced to withdraw Soul of the Matter with a career-ending ligament injury. Still, Mandella possessed a strong hand with Siphon and Dare and Go. Siphon, in particular, loomed as one to fear. Bill had sent Geri, a nice stakes horse owned by Allen, against Siphon in the Hollywood Gold Cup, only to watch that speedball scorch them after he seized an uncontested lead.

Bobby Frankel would again try us with Tinners Way, who had shown his affinity for Del Mar by winning the Pacific Classic each of the previous two years. Then there was Dramatic Gold, always troublesome with Nakatani in the irons.

When Bill and I consulted, we agreed we could not allow Siphon to shake loose, or the 1¼-mile contest might not be much of a contest. That thought was foremost on my mind—until we reached the starting gate, that is.

Cigar did not want to load.

While this may seem insignificant, it sounded as much of an alarm as the lack of burst at Arlington Park. When a horse who has always eagerly stepped behind the gate balks, that has to be his way of saying all is not right with his world.

I tapped him once, then the assistant starters coaxed him in.

My anxiety increased when Siphon, a one-time sprinter, instantly bolted to the front. *Got to get after him,* I thought.

As we took up the chase, Nakatani and Dramatic Gold rushed up outside of us, determined to push the pace even more.

Welcome to my worst nightmare. If I backed off, Siphon would go unchecked and history said he would not back up. If I continued to put the squeeze on Siphon while Dramatic Gold clung to us, there was no telling how fast the fractions might be.

I ride to win.

I never lose sight of that. If the streak was to end, someone would have to beat us. It would not happen because I had retreated when challenged.

Siphon would feel the heat. So would Dramatic Gold. I only hoped Cigar would not end up torched as well.

Siphon tore through the opening half mile in 45⅘ seconds. We were still there. So was Dramatic Gold.

Siphon blistered six furlongs in 1:09⅕, an impossible pace for the 1¼ miles but one conducive to a closer. We were a scant half-length behind. Nakatani kept the pedal down on Dramatic Gold.

Cigar finally passed a rubbery-legged Siphon on the turn for home. Dramatic Gold was cooked, too, as we blazed the mile in 1:33⅗ seconds.

But here came Dare and Go, a late-running 40–1 bomb with serious intentions.

Cigar had given me so much. Was there anything more?

I rapped him once.

Dare and Go went by.

I pleaded with Cigar.

No.

I was asking the impossible.

It was over.

I wrapped up as Dare and Go, having benefited from a wild pace that made the race for him, powered off to a three-and-a-half-length margin for fist-pumping Alex Solis. The final time of 1:59⅘ was only two-fifths of a second off the track record. That last eighth of a mile was the longest furlong I have ever ridden. I had never felt such emptiness.

Fans were stunned. They had come for a coronation, not an $81.20 payoff on a result that defied logic. Seventy-six percent of the win pool, or $1,163,588, had been wagered on Cigar with many of those tickets undoubtedly intended to become souvenirs. Now, they belonged in the trash.

I had never felt so torn.

After one flawless ride after another, had I made the best decision for Cigar?

There were only two of us out there. If anybody was going to be blamed for this staggering upset, I made sure it was not going to be him.

I think the press half-expected that I would be a no-show at the post-race news conference. As downcast as I was, I appreciated all the kind words written and spoken about Cigar in good times. At this very bad time, it would have been wrong for me to hold my tongue.

When you ride a horse like Cigar, a lot of other jockeys gun for you. They know where you are at all times. They look to float you outside, pin you against the rail, subtly impede you, do anything they possibly can to compromise your chances and keep the best horse from winning.

For fifteen consecutive races—Mike Smith piloted Cigar in an allowance win that started it all—I had kept my mount out of dire predicaments. I had not been able to avoid this one. I felt as if I had let everyone down, starting with Cigar.

I have replayed that race on my video recorder and in my mind hundreds of times. It is 1:59⅘ seconds of my life that never goes away. Each time, my conclusion is the same: Faced with a no-win situation, I did not win.

If I had dropped back, Siphon would have enjoyed a leisurely pace and Nakatani almost surely boxed me in with Dramatic Gold, a wrung-out victim of his own rider as he dragged home a distant fourth. As for the alternative, well, you know how that worked out.

Mandella, as always, was the epitome of class.

"I've got the utmost respect for Cigar and all he's accomplished," he said. "God knows I've tried hard enough to beat him. But the only way you keep a horse from getting beat is not run them. I've got to hand it to his people. They don't hide."

THERE WAS NO SECOND-GUESSING FROM BILL, WHOSE ability to keep Cigar at such a high level for so long represents one of the great training feats in history.

"It wasn't our day," he said simply.

BILL MOTT: *We thought Siphon was a pretty good horse. I had been out there earlier for the Hollywood Gold Cup with Geri and had run against Siphon. We let Siphon steal off by himself and never did catch him. The thing we failed to realize was that we didn't have Geri, we had Cigar.*

We also didn't count on Nakatani sacrificing his horse completely just to get us beat, and that's what he did. He gave his horse no chance.

He had no regard for the horse he was riding on, or the owner he was riding for, or the trainer he was riding for. He sacrificed everything to beat Cigar.

I went back to the barn with Suzee to commiserate with the rest of the team. Allen and Madeleine were as gracious as they could be. They were gratified just to know how much the horse had elevated the profile of his sport. They were confident the good times would roll again.

As always, I had tucked away a peppermint as a treat for Cigar. Normally, his ears pricked and he came right over for his favorite sweet as soon as he heard the cellophane being unwrapped.

This time, he balefully eyed the peppermint. He would not accept it when I opened the palm of my hand.

I don't know if he was mad at me or if he was just as despondent as I was. Either way, I understood. It wasn't exactly a peppermint day for me, either.

The end of the streak led to a natural debate. Which horse was better, Cigar or Citation? It is always difficult, if not impossible, to compare different generations in any sport. It is no different in mine.

I know Citation was an extraordinary animal and it would be wrong to say anything that might tarnish his legend. What I can say with conviction is that Cigar would have pushed to the breaking point any horse that was ever led to the starting gate.

With Allen having made the decision to retire the horse after the Breeders' Cup Classic, we wondered whether Cigar had won for the last time. How would he respond to the extremely taxing loss that had ended the streak?

Like a champion.

He was as full of vigor in his next start, the $500,000 Woodward Stakes on September 14, as he had ever been. A banner in the paddock read "Not In My House," and it was almost as if Cigar knew he was protecting his home course.

With L'Carriere, Smart Strike and Eltish all contributing to a solid but not crushing pace, I was able to give Cigar a stalking trip. His engine was purring, leaving no doubt he would take care of business. All I needed to do was tell him when.

He again made the lead after a mile, only this time we got there in 1:34⅗ seconds with one furlong left. We had gone the mile in 1:33⅗ at Del Mar with two furlongs to go.

That made all the difference between being a well-beaten second in the Pacific Classic and a commanding four-length victor against L'Carriere in the Woodward. Jorge Chavez, who rode L'Carriere, acknowledged that he never held much hope of holding on.

"Cigar, he was smoke," Chavez said.

Jorge was more accurate than he could have ever imagined. Like a puff of smoke that rises and disappears, we would not see Cigar at the top of his game in either of his last two races, the Jockey Club Gold Cup and the Breeders' Cup Classic.

Four-legged athletes are no different from the two-legged variety. The wear and tear of competition takes an inevitable toll. They lose a step or two or three. The demands of training and the pressure of racing can lead to mental burnout.

I suspect Cigar was feeling all of that as we neared the end. I will never forget his reaction when I pushed for more during a workout for the Gold Cup. He looked at me resentfully, as if to tell me he was traveling fast enough and that it was about time I left him alone.

The 1¼-mile Gold Cup brought a new and formidable challenger in three-year-old Skip Away, who would be facing older company for the first time. He was the main threat to us on paper, and, sure enough, he was the one to catch as I gave Cigar his cue on the turn for home.

My horse responded with what he had. I had ridden him perfectly. And yet it was not enough. We missed by a head to Skip Away. Much as it hurts me to acknowledge it, we were second best.

The torch was passed that day at Belmont Park, and everyone knew it. The joy of seeing a new star born was diminished by seeing Cigar's star begin to fade.

We went on to the Classic at Woodbine, driven more by a sense of obligation than any enthusiasm. Bill could see a substantial change in Cigar's training. The six-year-old had simply lost his edge.

I continued to be an optimist. Part of winning races is believing you can win. We had succeeded before when Cigar was not at the top of his game. I convinced myself we could grind it out one more time.

Cigar broke a step slow and was not tugging on me. That put us outside on a Woodbine track that definitely favored inside speed. I was forced to take him five wide at the head of the stretch

Cigar needed to produce the forceful move that had made him famous the world over. Like a puff of smoke, it was no longer there.

Alphabet Soup clipped Louis Quatorze by a nose. Cigar closed a head behind Louis Quatorze in third, putting his earnings at $9,999,815, a North American record.

There was talk of one more start for the sake of cracking $10 million. That lasted very briefly. This had been a class act all the way. No need to change now.

"I guess maybe it's time to go home," Allen said sadly.

And it was.

Allen had sold Cigar to Coolmore Stud for $25 million. Madeleine wanted to make sure there was a proper send-off. One week after his last race, she arranged for him to make a special appearance as part of the National Horse Show at New York's Madison Square Garden.

BILL MOTT: *I thought Madeleine Paulson was crazy for wanting to go to Madison Square Garden. It turned out to be one of the best*

*things we ever did. It is one of the most memorable, heartfelt things
I ever did.*

*Jerry and I both rode in the horse van. They blocked off the Lin-
coln Tunnel, which they don't even do for presidents. People lined
the streets a few blocks from Madison Square Garden.*

*Jerry gave up an afternoon of riding at Aqueduct. I asked him on
the way down, "Did you lose any live mounts?" He said, "Let me tell
you, I'm right where I want to be."*

*Jerry played a huge role. Cigar didn't have to overcome any bad
rides. He kept him out of trouble and gave him his best shot. He was
instrumental in the horse's success.*

Bill and I sat on bales of hay and reminisced throughout the van
ride from Queens to New York City. We both realized the horse
had transcended racing and touched people who had never seen a
Thoroughbred before. He had become a symbol of determination and excellence for a country and a world.

Track announcer Dave Johnson served as the emcee at Madison Square Garden and comedian Bill Cosby was on hand as well.
I had worried about how Cigar would react to the setting. He was
as calm and accommodating as a stable pony as we circled the
arena before I pointed him in every direction to acknowledge the
adulation of a crowd of more than sixteen thousand spectators.

A lone trumpet played "Auld Lang Syne."

There was nothing more to do after that except look forward
to Cigar's sons and daughters. Alas, that was not to be. He proved
to be infertile. I can understand why God would want him to be
one of a kind.

I had a passion for racing but not necessarily for Thoroughbreds when I entered the sport. I love Cigar. I make a point of visiting him each April at the Horse Park in Kentucky.

While he receives countless visitors each year, I'm quite sure he remembers me. In case he needs a reminder, I'm the one with the peppermints.

Thirteen

RISKY BUSINESS

*H*orses and racing, by their very nature, evoke strong emotions.

When you are a fan, you shake, you shout, you do everything you can to urge your horse home first. When you are part of the sport, you shake and shout for a very different reason. Much of the time, you want to scream in frustration.

Racing, it pains me to say, is far from reaching its potential. It is, in many respects, an ailing industry plagued by infighting, backward thinking and overall lack of vision.

This was clear to me as I served three-plus terms as president of the Jockeys' Guild, from December 1989 through 1996. Regrettably, nothing has changed since then. I fear for the future if the sport doesn't alter its course soon.

Upon Bill Shoemaker's retirement, the guild held a special election, and Chris McCarron and I both ran. I was gratified when my peers chose me. Unlike many past presidents who were mere figureheads, I took the position seriously. I was eager to devote time and effort on behalf of my generation and generations of riders to come.

While we made gains during my tenure, each involved a struggle. Sometimes, it came when least expected.

When someone suggested to me that jockeys should wear flak jackets to give their upper bodies some measure of protection, I thought it made perfect sense. I was quick to test different models in search of something light yet effective. Track managements soon embraced the idea because it would lower insurance premiums.

Judging by the reactions of a surprisingly large number of riders, however, you would have thought they were being asked to wear straitjackets. Some complained about added weight. Others claimed they were uncomfortable. Many simply didn't see the reason for change, a typical reaction in an industry that is rich in tradition but often seems hopelessly and needlessly bound to it.

I helped show my peers that flak jackets were potentially much more of a help than a hindrance when I wore one while piloting Black Tie Affair to victory in the 1991 Breeders' Cup Classic. I compare my experience with flak jackets to seat belts. There's lots of resistance at first, but after a while you feel much safer with it around you.

Make no mistake, fear is a passenger for some riders. Their actions give them away. If they have a golden position on the rail, they look for more open ground outside. They are not riding to win. They are striving to get around with the smallest amount of risk.

To my way of thinking, they should not be out there at all. They are like extremely slow drivers on a freeway. They make conditions worse for everyone.

Flak jackets did not eliminate the fear factor, but they did gradually gain acceptance. Through the years, a good number of jockeys have thanked me for introducing equipment that either saved their lives or kept them from more serious injury.

I wish I had been equally successful in my efforts to secure dramatically improved health and medical benefits. It wasn't for lack of trying.

I was prepared to lead a walkout at the start of 1995 in pursuit of that goal, only to be again reminded of how difficult it is to unite jockeys for any cause.

Athletes in major sports have shown they can come together when their financial futures are at stake. Perhaps because the individual struggle for live mounts and success is so great, jockeys have not been able to put petty jealousies and individual agendas aside for the common good. When that happens, you are ripe for exploitation.

We did not think it was asking too much when we sought one penny of every ten dollars wagered for improved medical benefits in an industry in which catastrophic injury may be a misstep away. Based on the resistance we encountered from the Thoroughbred Racing Association, you would have thought we were seeking ninety-nine cents from every dollar.

As hard as I worked to explain the justness of the cause to our members, breaks in the ranks could be detected as the January 1, 1995, walkout neared.

Several riders were set to take mounts in New York. Santa Anita was willing to permit my old friend Ray York, then sixty-one, to come out of retirement, as well as fifty-four-year-old Jerry Lambert. Calder was set to put on its card numerous has-beens and never-weres. Owners and trainers showed no regard for the job action by planning to enter the usual number of starters.

Gary Stevens spoke for many of the leading jockeys when he said, "I have no respect for the small riders who came and decided to ride. They said they have families to feed. We all have families to feed."

If we could not shut down the industry, we could not win.

It was time to make the best deal out there, and that's what we did on the eve of the scheduled stoppage. We gained an additional $150,000 to the approximately $1.7 million a year in per mount fees that had already gone to the guild. Medical and surgical coverage doubled, to $100,000. Accidental death and dismemberment protection increased from $5,000 to $25,000.

This was a case of well-established jockeys being willing to stand up for others who had not fared nearly so well—only to be sabotaged by those they were fighting to protect.

The fallout for me was severe. Three powerful stables blackballed me for a time. I know for a fact that the trainers of those outfits were told, "You will not ride Jerry Bailey."

After that, I am quite sure those in authority in the 1990s thought the issue of medical coverage would simply go away—but it is more pressing now than it has ever been.

In late 2004, the National Thoroughbred Racing Association asked me to join a panel of experts to examine the issue and make recommendations, after Gary Birzer, a jockey in West Virginia, was paralyzed in a devastating riding accident. Kelly Wietsma, my marketing representative, spearheaded an effort in which I was among those who donated five percent of his Breeders' Cup Day earnings to help Gary cope with massive medical expenses.

The gesture was helpful, but was only a Band-Aid—much more is needed in order to provide care for riders and those employed behind the scenes on the backside. There are several possible solutions, but I see a national workmen's compensation policy as the most viable. It will require compromise from all the various elements of a fragmented industry, including jockeys, horsemen and management. We have all acted in a me-me fashion long enough. It is time to put our differences aside, recognize that the whole is greater than the sum of its parts and do something that will ultimately serve all of us well.

When fans look at purse money being offered in major races and assume all jockeys are rich, they should think again. Racing cards at smaller tracks are composed of claiming races that carry relatively meager purses.

Beyond that, there are many hands that reach into the pot. The custom is for jockeys to receive ten percent of the money won. Out of that sum, he must pay taxes as well as twenty-five percent to his agent, five percent to his valet and two percent to grooms and exercise riders.

No one needs to pass the plate for the Bailey family, nor do I ask them to. I have topped the earnings list for a number of years now. I've never forgotten the words of my father, who drilled into me, "It's not what you make, it's what you end up with." With that in mind, I've made sound financial decisions through the years.

But I am incensed by people in this industry who think jockeys are overpaid. There are utility infielders who earn more than I do. There are NFL and NBA benchwarmers who make greater salaries.

And here I am at the top of my profession, taking on daily risks so great that it took two years to secure adequate health insurance for me and my family.

One of the sport's near-fatal flaws is that it views jockeys as, well, not a necessary evil but a necessary nuisance. I strongly suspect there are those in management who seek to suppress us rather than promote us.

Huge mistake. Think of where the NBA would be if it had not beaten the drums for Michael Jordan, Larry Bird and Magic Johnson. This industry has done itself a great disservice by not putting riders front and center.

Although everyone loves a good horse story, today's equine stars simply don't remain on the track long enough to have lasting marketing value.

Most breeders are intent on turning out precocious talent that features speed, speed, speed at the expense of durability.

To compound the problem, tracks resemble concrete freeways on the days of big races in an effort to put on a flashy show. Tracks invariably play a second or two faster for showcase events than they do for the rest of the meet.

And yet we are supposed to believe management doesn't do anything to enhance the surface? Come on. It occurs too often to be coincidental.

After that, the simple math of purse structure versus breeding value makes many top horses nothing more than shooting stars.

As soon as Smarty Jones put together the first two legs of the Triple Crown, owners Pat and Roy Chapman began investigating his breeding value even as they reiterated their desire to race him as a four-year-old. Insiders were not exactly surprised when he did not compete again after the Belmont Stakes.

While much hard work is done behind the scenes—we are all indebted to grooms and exercise riders—the two elements the public sees on the track are jockeys and horses. Elite riders maintain their position for a decade and more. Many of us have compelling stories. Horses don't stick around long. When I last checked, they can't talk.

Which would you promote?

It used to be that racing enjoyed a commanding position when it came to the gambling dollar. Not now. It is locked in an intense struggle with lotteries and casinos, not to mention jai alai, harness racing and dog racing.

And yet jockeys are treated as bit players and interchangeable parts. H. Allen Jerkens, the architect of many of racing's greatest upsets and a figure who commands the utmost respect, has seemingly spent his career trying to prove that riders make absolutely no difference.

That is simply not true. It would be like an owner choosing a trainer at random because they are all the same. No owner would ever do that.

Another example of the industry's disregard for riders is its insistence on maintaining a weight system that dates back to the nineteenth century. Some of us are doing irreparable harm to our long-term health, when allowing even a few more pounds would ease the burden.

In recent years, when asked what I am going to do when I retire, I developed a stock answer.

"I'm going to have lunch."

This has been my diet as a rider:

Breakfast: One English muffin or piece of toast with light mar-
garine. Coffee with cream. No sugar.

Lunch: One banana, eaten during the course of the day.

Dinner: One piece of meat, usually chicken. A salad and/or a
vegetable. One piece of red meat a month. Nothing other than
water for a beverage.

Still, kidney stones have been a problem for me during the lat-
ter part of my career. As painful as they have been, I am grateful
nothing worse occurred.

Randy Romero faces grave health issues stemming from a career
that extended from 1976 to 1999. He admits that he regularly
engaged in a practice known as "flipping." In other words, he used
his fingers to induce vomiting after eating. Many locker rooms
offer heaving bowls as a convenience. The taking of diuretics,
including one typically administered to horses, is not uncommon.

Randy once rubbed his body with alcohol and oil so he would
sweat profusely and shed as many calories as possible in a hot box
at Oaklawn Park in Arkansas. He caught fire when he brushed
against a lightbulb inside. He suffered second- and third-degree
burns over sixty percent of his body and narrowly escaped death.

We all wish he had paid more attention to good nutrition and
taken better care of himself while he competed. He has expressed those regrets as well.

Even racing must acknowledge that each generation is larger
and heavier than the one before. Something must be done to adjust
to that fact. I do not buy the argument from trainers that increased
weight means more horses will break down. These horses bear the
weight of exercise riders, some tipping the scale at 160 pounds,
morning after morning. No one worries about that.

Owners and trainers who truly care about the well-being of horses, not to mention the health of the sport, would do well to focus on identifying and punishing those who use illegal medications. Everyone knows they are out there, although I don't know the specifics as to what is done and how widespread the practice is.

If jockeys had their way, horses would run on nothing more than hay, oats and water. If that was the case, horses would simply stop running when they began to experience discomfort in a certain part of their bodies.

When pain is masked, accidents occur, possibly resulting in paralysis or death for jockeys. I cannot say for certain which barns cheat. Sometimes you see a horse's form improve so dramatically in a new trainer's hands that it just doesn't add up.

I have always stayed away from those kinds of situations. Even then, it takes only one illegally medicated horse in a race to cause a tragedy that lasts a lifetime.

I know it is difficult to catch those who cheat, but a huge effort is needed to make advances in this area. Currently, there are trainers who would prefer to run clean horses but get caught up in veterinary chicanery merely because they feel it is necessary to keep up with the competition. Trainers who endure prolonged slumps tend not to be trainers very long. Owners want results. Let's face it, most of them don't ask questions about how they are achieved.

On a good note, I believe race fixing is largely an ugly thing of the past. I cannot say with certainty that it never happens, and I've already related how I was approached when I rode in Detroit early in my career.

In the last twenty years, however, I have not heard of, or witnessed, any instance of race fixing. Decades ago, trainers desperate to pay bills often saw it as the only way out. With improved purse structures, boosted by the installation of slot machines in many states, that is no longer the case. For riders on major circuits, I cannot conceive of a fixer being able to pay enough money to make it worthwhile for a jockey to risk everything by stiffing a mount.

When suspicion briefly arose that José Santos might have carried a buzzer when he urged Funny Cide to victory in the Kentucky Derby in 2003, that was laughable. There must be eight television cameras and eighty still cameras focused on you at all times. A person would have to be insane to think he could carry an electrical device to stimulate a Derby horse and not be detected. Of course, José was exonerated.

With Funny Cide falling short of the Triple Crown after winning the first two legs in 2003 and Smarty Jones narrowly missing by one length in 2004 to extend the longest drought in history, there has been increased talk that perhaps the format should be changed.

Three races at different distances at different tracks in five weeks exerts enormous physical and mental pressure on still-developing three-year-olds. It is safe to say many potentially great horses are compromised by the ordeal.

That is the basis for the argument that perhaps spacing between races should be increased while the distance of the 1½-mile Belmont Stakes be decreased.

In this case, I say don't mess with history. Let's not tread on more than a century of tradition when it comes to the Kentucky Derby, Preakness and Belmont Stakes. Let the Triple Crown continue to stand for what it is—arguably the greatest accomplishment in all of sports.

Otherwise, change absolutely must come to racing, in the area of promotion and in the way it treats horses and human beings. We can, and must, do better.

Fourteen

LIVING TO WIN

*I*n 1995, I was elected to the Racing Hall of Fame on the first ballot. As I sat at the induction ceremony in the glorious August sunshine, I struggled to absorb all that had transpired.

Losing my mother, who would have been so proud. Losing years of potential brilliance to drunken nights. Finding Suzee, whose unrequited love and dedication ultimately changed everything. Finding sobriety, and with that clarity of vision, finding that I could be great.

It all felt like a dream that day at Saratoga Springs, New York. But it was my dream, and it had come true.

There was Mack Miller, who had rehired me a short time after he had let me go, presenting me for induction.

"He's one of the finest riders in America, and he's my close friend," Mack said. The second half of the sentence meant as much to me as the first.

There was my plaque, which read:

The skill and finesse of Jerry Bailey were vividly illustrated on the 1991 weekend he got Hansel home by a head in the Belmont Stakes on Saturday and Meadow Star home by a nose in the Mother Goose Stakes the next day. Bailey also had ridden that pair to victories in the Preakness and Acorn Stakes, respectively. Son of a Texas dentist, Bailey became a Quarter Horse rider at the age of 12, then began in Thoroughbred racing in 1974. Into 1995, his mounts had earned more than $100 million and he rode seven winners on Florida Derby Day that year at Gulf-stream Park. Bailey, an outspoken president of The Jockeys' Guild, was the leading rider on various occasions at Belmont Park, Keeneland, Hawthorne, and Calder. By 1995, his legion of major triumphs included three Breeders' Cup Classics already in the 1990's—on Black Tie Affair, the 133–1 Arcangues, and Concern. He also won the Kentucky Derby and Travers Stakes in 1993 on Sea Hero. Bailey partnered Fit to Fight through his New York Handicap Triple Crown sweep of 1984, and his other mounts include Cigar, Sultry Song, Proper Reality, You'd be Surprised, Time for a Change, Fly So Free, Candy Éclair, and Fraise. Inducted 1995.

I was flooded with memories of all the mornings Mack and I had conversed over coffee. How special they were. "Mack Miller showed me the right way," I told the crowd as I fought back tears.

Singer/songwriter Burt Bacharach, a Thoroughbred owner,

performed a medley of his hits as part of the ceremony. As he concluded, strains of "That's What Friends Are For" drifted into the sweet summer air.

Perfect. So much of my story is about how indispensable family, and a few good friends, are.

MY SISTER KATHY: *I do love him with all my heart. I can't tell you how proud I am of him because I know the dedication this has taken. He has given his whole life for this.*

MY SISTER BECKY: *He's the person I always knew he was. Perhaps alcohol masked that personality, but he's back to the person I always knew was inside—caring, genuine, a hard driver.*

Once he sets his mind to something, there is no stopping him. He is going to do what he says he's going to do.

MY FATHER, JIM: *Suzee has an awful lot to do with Jerry's success. She's the one who pulled him out of the gutter. Had she not had the tenacity to stick with a drunk and help him get over his addiction, Jerry would never have matured to do what he's done.*

SUZEE'S PARENTS, FRAN AND JACK: *We are so proud of our son-in-law, not only for the success he's had on the track but for the changes he's made as a person. We could not ask for a better husband for our daughter or a better father for our grandson.*

Suzee saw qualities in Jerry years ago that made her want to fight for him and made her want to spend the rest of her life with him. We admit we did not initially see those qualities. We thank God that her judgment was right.

MY BEST FRIEND BRYAN FANN: *When I think back on those nights out, it was crazy. It was crazy. I stopped drinking three years ago and Jerry was instrumental. He was there when I needed him. In fact, he was the first person I called when I decided it was time for me to stop.*

I was lucky to have somebody like him to help me when I needed to do something. He was there all the way.

He once said to me, "Man, did you ever think I would do this good?" I said, "No, I didn't." The ability was always there. I just didn't think he had the drive.

We laugh about the old days, but neither of us miss them. We are happy to be where we are. Racing would have missed a real star without Jerry Bailey. I'm just glad things worked out for him.

I was inducted that day along with Bobby Frankel, a trainer with whom I would accomplish much later on, and the equine stars Foolish Pleasure, La Prevoyante and Crusader.

An interview with the *Thoroughbred Times* led me to reflect on qualities that were allowing me to succeed beyond my wildest imagination.

"Assuming you have all the physical attributes you need—size, weight, strength and balance—you have to have a skin made of cowhide," I told the interviewer. "This is a very humiliating business and a very unforgiving one. It's got its great rewards, but if you want a lesson in humility, just stay around the racing game a little while.

"What it has taught me is to always keep trying. I think Shoemaker's win percentage was twenty-five percent or so. He was losing three out of four. So in a game when you're at the top of the pile by losing three out of four, it gives you a sense of determination and a sense of the motto 'Don't ever give up.' "

Believe me, racing knocks you down, many times in many ways, but I always jumped to my feet immediately. As much as I questioned whether I could have done anything differently in the controversial end to Cigar's massive winning streak, I never allowed doubt to be part of my game. The greats find something extra when it means the most, and I was able to do that.

RON ANDERSON, MY AGENT FROM APRIL 2000 UNTIL THE PRESENT: *People who don't understand our industry ask me, "How good is he?"*

He's the Michael Jordan of racing, that's who he is.

He can consistently be on the second-, third- or fourth-best animal and win. He outthinks everybody a lot of the time. When he gets to the paddock, he's got three or four different scenarios already worked out in his head. When something happens and everybody else is surprised, he's prepared for it in some shape or form.

I think he really gets psyched for the big days. He really gets into it. I think it's an adrenaline situation, a preparation of mind where he can completely dissect a situation in a race.

He knows what he wants to do and can do. He knows what everybody else wants to do or can do. It's a complex puzzle, but he figures it out probably like no one else.

That first journey to Dubai with Cigar was only the beginning of my World Cup success. I would enhance my reputation as one of the finest money riders of all time by delivering World Cup triumphs with Singspiel (1997), Captain Steve (2000) and Street Cry (2002).

The last two were particularly special because Suzee and Justin were both there, and it helped Justin understand the magnitude of some of the events I was involved in.

JUSTIN: *It was an awesome feeling to know my father rode the best horse in the world. It was an awesome moment when he won.*

The rest of the time there was a blast. Riding a camel in the desert. Making moves with my Boogie board on the sand dunes. Throwing a football with Dad. The thing I liked most about Dubai, they serve french fries instead of bread at the restaurants.

When Cigar was retired, I could not help but wonder where my career would go from there. While he could not be replaced, my success continued at a rate that would reach record proportions.

After Cigar, I would get a leg up on 1998 Horse of the Year Skip Away, who won seven of nine graded stakes that season. After Cigar, I would capture eight more Breeders' Cup races to become the all-time leader with fourteen, lifting my career earnings above $265 million with more than 5,500 wins.

When Jerry Bailey bobbleheads were distributed at Saratoga on the last Saturday of July 2002, I was able to present my fans with something else—eight winners, four on each day of the weekend.

In the new millennium, my sternest competition came from within. In 2002, I finished with 213 victories, 67 stakes wins capped by Orientate's sizzling performance in the Breeders' Cup Sprint, earnings of $19,271,814 and a record-tying sixth Eclipse award.

Just when I thought it could not possibly get any better, 2003 came along. I broke my own records with $23.35 million in earnings and seventy stakes triumphs, including what was widely viewed as an impeccable ride to bring Six Perfections home first in the Breeders' Cup Mile and Empire Maker's brilliant Belmont Stakes performance to thwart Funny Cide's Triple Crown bid.

That yielded an unprecedented seventh Eclipse, one more than the mark I had shared with Laffit Pincay. Laffit's total includes a special Eclipse in 1999 to commemorate his breaking of Shoemaker's all-time record for wins.

As much as I treasured all my accomplishments, however, in recent years I have felt family life tugging on me harder than Cigar ever could. The loneliness of the road became more severe. Cell phone conversations were as troubling as they were comforting because nothing replaces being there.

I honored all my commitments, as I always have, but I cut back on my riding schedule so I could spend more time with Suzee—my wife, my confidante, my everything—and with Justin.

I have gone to great lengths to see even a few innings of Justin's baseball games, not because I necessarily envision him as a future major league infielder but simply because a father should be there for his son. To see him succeed, or even to see him fail but try hard in the attempt, gives me great joy.

To play him one-on-one in basketball, to share our passion for the New York Yankees by watching a game together, to sit and ask him about his day at school—these activities, as mundane as they may sound, are special to us. I do not want to look back and realize that my child became a man and I was not around to accompany him on that journey.

JUSTIN: *When I was young, I didn't understand why Dad was not there helping to coach the team. I really missed him. Especially in the fall, he could never make any of my games.*

My mom had to be like my dad, cheering me on and stuff. I

started to understand that he was away because he was a famous athlete, but he's always been just Dad when we're at home. When we go to the track and people say, "What an awesome job your father did!" that's when I realize that he means a lot to other people, too.

While I know my son must make his own decisions, I am teaching him as he approaches his teenage years that all decisions have consequences. If he chooses to drink and drive, or is a passenger of a driver who had too much to drink, the consequences can be horrific.

I must be there to tell him why I have faith in God, why I converted to Catholicism in 1999 after years of spiritual bankruptcy. I had grown up a Methodist but when my father moved away from that faith, I did the same.

I am not an in-your-face person when it comes to religion. But I know my faith in God sustained me throughout my life's journey, and I would be nowhere without it.

Without that faith and God-given ability, I could not have dominated my era the way I did. Without that faith and God-given ability, I could not have surpassed Cordero (640 victories) in 2004 for most career wins at prestigious Saratoga Race Course.

Without our shared faith, Suzee and I could not have saved our marriage. Suzee and I devoted countless hours to counseling, to communicating without the help of a third party, to putting the pieces of our marital puzzle back together. Through it all, we felt God's guiding hand was joined with ours.

SUZEE: *We don't have the prescription for a perfect marriage. With all of our failings as human beings, I am not sure a perfect marriage exists.*

I can say we never take each other for granted anymore. We have gained a lot more respect for each other, and with that comes a deeper love. We do things for each other for all the right reasons now, not to avoid an argument.

We work at our marriage. We find what works that day and look for a better tomorrow, never sure of what that might bring.

When you are married to an alcoholic, friends always ask, "Are you worried that your husband will drink again?" There were times in the first few years when I would wonder, "Is he?" But through Al-Anon meetings and my faith, I learned to let it go.

Jerry will always be an alcoholic. At any given time he could drink. I've had to accept that. I've learned to live for today, and today is beautiful. Enjoy it for all it's worth.

I believe God put my wife and others in my path to help me when I was at the bottom of my ocean. When all around me was darkness, they pointed toward a ray of light. Then it was up to me to kick as hard as I could.

Like all alcoholics, I remain without a cure but with tremendous hope. As of this writing, it has been more than sixteen years since my last drink. My thirst is gone.

Sobriety is too good, the simple pleasures of family life too fulfilling, for me to want to consume a depressant.

Still, I continue to attend at least one Alcoholics Anonymous meeting a week, to help others as they continue to help me. Long after I end one of the most illustrious careers in racing history, it will never be in my nature to back off in any endeavor.

I ride to win.

I live to win.

ACKNOWLEDGMENTS

First of all, I would like to thank God, for without your blessings of talent and perseverance, none of the great things in my life would have been possible.

Thank you, God.

I would like to thank my mother, Betty, may she rest in peace, and my father, James. Without their love and support, I may never have made it through those "I'm too small" years.

My friends at Coronado High were instrumental in my happy and smooth high school experience, and I am forever grateful for all of them. But I would be remiss if I didn't single out Kevin Baker, my best school buddy. Kevin was the star running back on the football team, and one of the most popular guys in school. Whatever the event or party, Kevin made sure I was always included. Thanks, Kevin.

I would have to say that the majority of my teachers and coaches in school were the kind that made coming to school fun for me. I do, however, want to give a special thanks to grade school coach Dubb White.

Coach White, realizing I was too small for the football team, made me head manager, so in some way I could still be part of the team.

Since the racetrack was my other life, let me try to thank all those who lent a helping hand not only to my success, but to my survival:

My father must again receive some accolades, since he served as my first agent, booking mounts for me when no other agent would take me seriously enough. Thanks to all the other agents who helped my career onward and upward, in the best chronological order I can remember: Chuck Sherman, who could have been my agent today had he wished, that's how much I think of his talent. I think Chuck preferred to live in the Northwest. Bill Shuman, a good agent, but a better human being. Bill and his wife, Betty, served as surrogate parents at a time when I really needed them—thank you both. Fred Aimie and Doc Danner both handled my business in Kentucky. I was probably more aggravation than anything else to them at that time, but they had me winning at a high percentage, and I am still friends with both. Jesse Parsons, who worked for me in Florida and also did a fine job. John Dale, who was my first New York agent and represented me from 1982 until 1984. We were a good fit for each other during that time. Bob Frieze, who took over for me in 1984 and helped me rise to the top of the rankings; together we won three jockey championships, all three Triple Crown races and many Breeders' Cup races. But as much as anything, we stayed together through the final years of my drinking and managed to get through to the successful years. Thanks, Bob.

And finally Ron Anderson, who is without a doubt the most intelligent and savvy agent of any era. One major difficulty of handling a top rider is picking the best of many choice mounts, without offending anyone. Ron seems to have a great knack in that area. Ron went to work for me in 2000. My business was tailing off a bit, and I thought I still had some productive years ahead of me. Well, Ron delivered from the start. The first four years with Ron, we won four championships. Perfection!

If I had not broken my arm in September 2004, we might have won a fifth. Thanks, Ron.

To all the owners and trainers who helped my career, I wish to thank you all. I would, however, like to name a few: Joe and Barbie Allbritton, Allen Paulson, Sheikh Mohammed bin Rashid Al Maktoum, Mike Pegram, Bob and Janice McNair, Paul Mellon, Jeff Sullivan, Sonny and Caroline Hine, Bill Clifton, Bill Young, Ogden Phipps, Bob and Beverly Lewis, Satish and Anne Sanan, Charlotte Weber, Ed Gann, Prince Khalid Abdullah, Russell Reineman, Frank Stronach, Bob and Bonnie Holthus, Wayne Lukas, Joe Orseno, Tommy Albertrani, Bob Baffert, Bobby Frankel, Shug McGaughy and Ray Spencer.

Neal and Arnold Winick, who brought me from Chicago to Florida in 1976 and gave me instant credibility in top-class racing.

Mack Miller, who not only provided me with a plethora of top stakes horses to ride, but was also a trusted friend. I rode for Mack and Paul Mellon's Rokeby Stable from 1982 until the stable dispersal in 1994 (with a year hiatus, of course). My association with Mack was instrumental in my success in New York for a couple of reasons. One, he was very respected; if you were good enough for Mack, you were good enough for most everyone. Two, riding for Mack meant top stakes horses to ride every week, every year. Thanks, Mack!

Bill Mott. Nobody, I mean nobody, was as loyal as both a trainer and a friend as Bill Mott. Not to mention one of the best horsemen of our generation. I was fortunate to start riding for Bill shortly after the dispersal of Rokeby Stable in 1994, and coincidentally that was the same year Cigar hit the scene. But Cigar was not the only good horse in Bill's barn. The list of top stakes horses went on and on. One great thing about Bill's horses, they lasted more than one season because he managed them so well. I have ridden for Bill from 1994 until the writing of this book, a length of time together unheard of in this business. I believe the one thing that made the relationship last is that I trusted him, and he trusted me. There were never any jealousies or competition for the limelight. Bill and I always understood that you can't win 'em all. One thing that can break up a successful trainer-jockey combo is when a jock continually jumps off the stable mount to ride for another trainer with a "hot horse." Bill, unlike a lot of other trainers, was very understanding in these matters. Bill would almost never keep me from riding a good horse for someone else, even if it meant not riding his. Bill, you're the best! Thanks.

I would also like to thank all the grooms and exercise riders of all the horses I've ever ridden. Their tireless work and countless hours of dedication sometimes go unappreciated and unknown. You guys should get more of the glory! I thank you all.

I WOULD BE REMISS IF I DID NOT SAY THANKS TO ALL OF THE valets who have worked for me across the country since I began riding in 1974. A valet is responsible for saddling our horses in all the races we ride, as well as maintaining all of our equipment. Their title describes their job fairly accurately. They hang our clothes when we arrive, provide us with toiletries, keep water and snacks available for us between races, go for this, go for that—basically they service us with everything we might need from the time we arrive before the races until we are finished. I must single out two men who worked for me for more than twenty-two years—Buddy Hasher in Florida and Eddie Brown in New York. Each was not only my valet but also a good friend who put up with more temper tantrums, complaining, and just plain childish bullcrap from me than any human should. (Did I mention that I wasn't always a pleasant loser?) Thanks, guys, you were a big part of my longevity.

On numerous issues in racing, jockeys and management fall on different sides of the proverbial fence. More often than not, management does not have the best interest of the jockeys foremost in their mind, and that can create conflicts, infighting, and hard feelings. However, there are a few men in management who always took the time to try and see issues from a jockey's perspective. Although these men did not always agree, they went the extra mile, and sometimes it made the difference: Kenny Noe, Terry Meyocks, Lou Raffetto, Corey Johnson, Dick Duchossois, William Thayer, Kenny Dunn and Chick Lang, Jr. Thanks, gentlemen.

My friends:

I have had many acquaintances in my life, but only a few friends. I would like to mention two in particular. Gary Young has been a friend since we met in South Florida in 1976. We lived in the same apartment complex, and as we both worked for the Winick family, we often shared a ride to work. Although we have lived on opposite coasts for years, we speak almost daily. Gary has always been a person who tells it like it is, and he has always told me the truth. As fickle as racetrackers can be, Gary has always been in my corner. Thanks, Uncle G.

Bryan Fann is one of only two friends I have had from the jockey colony. The other was Don MacBeth, who died from cancer in 1987 at the age of thirty-five. It is not that I don't like or get along with almost all the riders in America, it's just very hard to develop real friendships with guys who are taking your mounts and vice versa. But somehow Bryan and I remained good friends throughout—he was even the best man at my wedding. Bryan was always a straight shooter, and put up with more of my crap in the drinking days than the law allowed, I will cherish his friendship.

My family:

My sister Becky, whose unconditional love will be appreciated always. Becky seemed to be the caretaker of the family after Mom died.

She was the one who held the family together—we needed that. She always kept in touch, and was the one I could count on if I ever needed anything. All I had to do was ask. When I broke my jaw in 1976 in a riding mishap, she was on the first plane to Miami. Thanks for everything, Becky!

My little sister, Kathy. We were the closest growing up, only thirteen months apart in age. One of the things I admire about Kathy is her free spirit. She was the first to get married and left the nest at an early age, as I did, and never looked back. She, too, kept close tabs on my racing career, and never failed to let me know how proud she was of me.

My dad. Although I touched on him briefly earlier, I would like to expound a little more. I know he had an extremely difficult time after Mom died, especially after we kids left to find lives of our own. I can only imagine how lonely he felt. Although he has never been one to wear his heart on his sleeve, I know that he loves me and is proud of my accomplishments. I love you, Dad!

My in-laws, Jack and Fran Chulick. They must have been in quite a turmoil watching their daughter marry an active alcoholic. Fortunately, things worked out okay. I am as close to them as I am to my own family. Thanks for all your support of Suzee and me. I hope I have come through for you.

Justin. You have been a dream son. Not only do you make me proud on a daily basis, but you have been very understanding about all the things in your life that I have missed because of my traveling. Sometimes I think that instead of me teaching you about life, you have taught me. I enjoy watching all your sporting events, but most of all, I enjoy watching you grow into a fine man. I love you, son.

Ahhhh!!! Suzee, you are the love of my life, and my best friend. You have always seen things in me that I could not see in myself. I can't put into words how much I appreciate your being there and being there and being there for me. You were there for me when I was not there for you, and not one complaint. You helped me get through some rock-bottom times, and helped me appreciate the good ones. You have been a tremendous mother to Justin and, when I was traveling, a father as well. You have been a source of inspiration and a pillar of strength, more than you could possibly know. Although at times you might have questioned your choice in me, your love never wavered, nor did mine. I couldn't have done it without you. Thanks, and I love you!

IN ORDER FOR A STORY LIKE THIS TO TAKE LIFE ON PAPER, IT takes a great deal of effort by many people. I would like to thank the following people for all their hard work.

Tom Pedulla. Thanks for all your hard work and many hours with me and my family in preparing this project. Your good humor and willingness to go to any lengths to get things right made it a pleasure, not a chore. Well done, Tom.

Neil Nyren. Neil, your advice throughout the writing of this book was invaluable. Your diligence and attention to detail was more than I could have expected. Thanks.

Kelly Wietsma. You probably put more hours into this book than anyone. Your coordination of everything from A to Z was nothing short of amazing. I owe your family a big thank-you for sharing you for all these months. I can't thank you enough for all your hard work. You're the best.

Barbara Livingston. Your beautiful images have captured so much of my career. Thanks for all of your help and support!

Harold Roth. Thanks for going that extra mile to help us out.

—Jerry Bailey